THE
SAFE ROOM

A Guide for School Crisis Responders

CHERI LOVRE

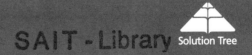

Solution Tree

Cover art and design by Grannan Graphic Design Ltd.
Text design by T. G. Design Group
Printed in the United States of America
ISBN 1-932127-81-X

Dedication

This book is dedicated to the memory of Jovita Reyes, who lived courageously and struggled valiantly with cancer in her young life. In the early years of her treatment for leukemia, she gave presentations in her classrooms to reassure her elementary school peers that what she had was not contagious and that she was going to be okay. In her teenage years, she awed us with her beauty at the formal dance at cancer camp and charmed us as she danced with us from her motorized chair.

Other Resources
by Cheri Lovre

Administrator's Grab and Go Briefcase

All Staff Preparedness Training Package

Catastrophic Events Resource Manual

Crisis Resource Manual

Emergency Kit CD

Grab and Go Duffel

Media Relations for Educators

Reclaiming Life! A Workbook for Survivors of Trauma

The Day That . . . A Workbook for Youth in the Aftermath of Trauma

Visit the Crisis Management Institute (CMI) web site at www.cmionline.org for other materials and more information about crisis training. As a service to schools, CMI posts guidelines for administrators, counselors, teachers, and parents in the aftermath of major events. These are free to download and distribute, as long as the copyright information is left intact at the bottom of every page.

Acknowledgments

This book has been years in the making, in terms of my gaining experience and having the opportunity to respond to a wide variety of school tragedies.

I am indebted to Karen Johnston, who worked closely with me in the early years of facilitating school responses when we both worked for Marion Education Services District (now Willamette ESD) in Salem, Oregon. Karen first identified the value of making one person responsible for spearheading and fostering the development of the Safe Room, and she has graciously stepped up to the plate time and time again, creating safe havens of warmth for thousands of students in the past 20 years. Her insights continually enhanced our abilities and improved our process.

Karen, no matter where I go, I think of you each time I walk into a Safe Room environment.

Table of Contents

About the Author

Cheri Lovre, M.S., is a nationally recognized expert in school crisis and trauma response and prevention with more than 25 years of experience assisting schools in the aftermath of tragedy.

She provides crisis response training and technical assistance to a variety of emergency services agencies, victim advocacy groups, trauma responders, and employee assistance providers. Her former clients include the National Association of Secondary School Principals, the American School Counselors Association, the National Association of School Psychologists, and the Association of Educational Service Agencies.

Ms. Lovre developed the LOVRE model for trauma intervention, a philosophy and approach addressing the unique needs of students and staff in the aftermath of events that may lead to acute trauma. She is the founder and director of the Crisis Management Institute in Salem, Oregon.

Preface

There is no way around it: Unfortunately, experience is by far the best teacher for improving one's ability to help others through grief. Each experience will present new obstacles and challenges. Nothing in the world of crisis is black and white, and the same principle applies to running Safe Rooms. Simply put, this book offers guidelines—important ones, but guidelines nonetheless.

There is very little in the way of formal education, school counseling, or school psychology programs that can emotionally prepare educators for the kinds of school crises they face today. I hope, however, this book will be helpful on a practical level to counselors, school psychologists, school social workers, school nurses, and crisis team members, as well as administrators, teachers, and parents. As you look at Safe Rooms—the structure, the process, and the training—consider that the philosophy, skill, and pragmatism used there have applications that span a wide spectrum of human experiences.

I hope you find value in this information beyond your professional role to include your other roles—as parent, partner, neighbor, relative, and friend. Bless you for giving to others as they walk the path toward healing.

Chapter 1

The Safe Room Concept

Those of us in the "bifocal stage" of life can remember a time when, if a student died, his or her classmates might attend the funeral, but would not receive special support at school. Schools did not know how to support the grief process. In the 1960s and 1970s, it was common to hear school staff remark that students would grieve best with their families, at home.

Today, we know much more about the grief process. One important revelation is that we grieve best with those who shared a relationship with the deceased similar to our own. This means that those who were in the same classes, played on the basketball team, or were in the school play with the deceased student cope best when they grieve together in the natural groupings in which they knew the student. The death will have special meaning for these students; by grieving together, they will learn crucial lessons and build coping skills that will last a lifetime.

A Place Set Aside

The Safe Room is an outgrowth of our new knowledge about grief and trauma. Simply put, the Safe Room is a temporary space where students who are most bereft after a tragedy, crisis, or loss can receive additional support. The primary focus of the Safe Room is to give students an opportunity to learn about, process, and find the meaning of the loss for themselves, often through talking with peers in small groups or engaging in activities with trained staff members. The crisis may be a large-scale event such as a school shooting or natural catastrophe that claimed many lives, or it may be the death of a single student due to illness, suicide, an accident, or homicide.

Whatever the crisis may be, once the Safe Room is open, students can visit it before, during, or after class to talk with their peers and with trained staff. The Safe Room is open to all grieving students, including those grieving deaths and life events unrelated to the current crisis. In the Safe Room, students begin to come to terms with their own grief, learn to accept and support others who are grieving, and come together to *do* something that gives the death meaning.

While teachers will likely encourage students to express and share their grief within individual classrooms, the Safe Room provides additional support to those students who are most bereft and cannot focus on normal academic tasks. In the immediate aftermath of tragedy, the Safe Room is a quiet space set aside; it serves the needs of grieving students and allows less affected students to move on in the classroom. Later, all students can gather for a memorial ritual or ceremony, referred to as a "memory event" in this resource.

In some cases it is necessary to have more than one Safe Room because of the number of students in need. Sometimes the layout of the school dictates that students visit the Safe Room closest to their classrooms; other times it may be helpful to separate students by grade level. Additionally, when staff members are more affected by an event than students—for example, if a teacher commits suicide—a staff Safe Room may also be appropriate to allow teachers and administrators to grieve together.

The Safe Room is just one critical part of the overall school crisis response. Ideally, when a school provides a Safe Room, it also provides training on grief support for counseling staff. In addition, crisis response should include a broad range of services and activities that complement the Safe Room function. This book assumes that as part of crisis response strategy, a school may have a designated Rapid Response Team: an in-house, "local" team trained to provide first aid, direct students, and lead the immediate response in a crisis.

The local team does not operate the Safe Room, however. Local school teachers and counselors will be needed to maintain their regular roles within the school; local school administrators will have more immediate responsibilities in a crisis. Instead, an outside crisis response team consisting of staff, counselors, and teachers from other schools—called the Flight Team in this resource— "flies in" to provide assistance. Flight Team members help administrators and staff cope and assume other roles as needed—*including operating the Safe Room.* Chapter 2 (page 11) will provide more detail on the technical side of staffing and running the Safe Room; for now, please simply note that the Safe Room should be one part of a larger crisis response plan.

It is important to understand that activating your own Rapid Response Team, calling in and briefing the Flight Team on the specifics of your school, and opening a Safe Room should not call attention to individual crisis responders, however highly trained they may be. The public should not see news reports of "expert" assistance being called in for "disturbed" children. A Safe Room puts the school in the best possible light during a critical period by showing the community that the school cares about its students. A Safe Room is not a kind of mental health emergency center where experts examine and diagnose children in a clinical setting; instead, it is a soothing, flexible environment where approachable staff members can ask gentle, informal questions to guide children through the grieving process and to determine which children, if any, might need long-term assistance.

Common Misconceptions

Administrators and staff may raise objections to establishing a Safe Room. These are often based on some common misconceptions about the purpose and management of a Safe Room.

Misconception 1: Students will not talk with people they do not know. The goal of the Safe Room is not to provide professional adult counsel to individual grieving students (although that option should be included), but rather to provide a comfortable environment where students can grieve with *each other*.

One of the primary tasks of grieving for youth is to share their loss through activities such as sharing memories, planning the memory event, writing cards and letters to the family, and participating in other activities. The adults in the Safe Room simply encourage students to grieve together and ensure that they learn to speak about the loss in hopeful terms rather than surrender to negative emotional reactions.

When a student *does* want to talk with an adult, however, he or she is more likely to self-disclose or think out loud to a compassionate adult who does not know the student or the student's family and history. When a child discloses abuse, mentions thoughts of suicide, or shows other signs of being at risk, referral to the school counselor is crucial. For that reason, the Safe Room staff needs to be well-trained even though only a minority of students will need one-to-one support from an adult.

In light of students' need for privacy, comfort, and safety, implement a policy that parents will not be permitted in the Safe Room. While they may want to help, they can actually disrupt the process. Remember, the goal of the Safe Room is to provide a comforting environment where students can openly process their grief with their peers. Having the parents of other students around can be intimidating and may cause students to limit their emotional expression. This may prevent them from making critical disclosures of suicidal thoughts or abuse. Further, permitting one parent in the Safe Room means allowing *any* parent. Most school administrators and counselors can identify at least a few parents they absolutely would not want in the Safe Room.

For the most part, students simply want adults who will listen and allow them to process their loss.

Misconception 2: Providing a Safe Room makes a bigger deal out of an event. Grief is a natural response to the loss of a loved one. By allowing those students who need extra time for processing the loss to temporarily leave the academic environment, the Safe Room greatly assists the teaching process in the rest of the school. The Safe Room enables teachers to return to academics when most of their students are ready, instead of having to stop the lesson to comfort the few students who are deeply troubled.

Misconception 3: Students will use the Safe Room just to get out of classroom work. Actually, many students use the Safe Room because they have unrelated and sometimes unresolved issues that have surfaced because of the unstable emotional climate created by the crisis. For that reason, teachers should avoid being gatekeepers and should release all students who voice an interest in going to the Safe Room. Those students who are truly affected may be unable to work in class, and Safe Room staff will send back any students who are not working on valid emotional issues.

Misconception 4: Students should only spend one class period in the Safe Room and then return to class. Some will need even less than a full class period, but many will need more time. Each child should be allowed to use the room as long as needed.

Initial Steps

Take the following initial steps to ensure that the Safe Room is integrated into your school's crisis response plan.

1. Gain administrative support for the Safe Room concept. Encourage administrators across the district (or across all districts, if collaborating) to use and trust the team process required for Safe Room implementation.

2. Develop school policy. An effective policy outlines how crises will be handled, what level of training the in-house Rapid Response Team and the visiting Flight Team members must receive, who those people are, how they are contacted, and other critical elements of activating teams once they are in place.

3. Identify a representative staff. Be sure that the demographics of the staff in the Safe Room mirror the cultural and ethnic groups likely to use the Safe Room. We grieve and process best when the people who provide our support look like someone who could be related to us or could be a member of a social group that includes our family. This can mean bringing in paraprofessionals who are bilingual, who share the same ethnic backgrounds as students, or who are familiar classroom aides.

4. Obtain specific training for Safe Room staff. Avoid assuming that counselors will do a great job because of their background. Much organization and training are needed to support and prepare Safe Room staff. Safe Room skills are different than traditional counseling skills. Some people who will do very well in the Safe Room will be those who ordinarily have roles other than counseling but who have a talent for working with children in emotional pain.

5. Identify the location for the Safe Room. Carefully consider the space required for the Safe Room. It must be private, comfortable, easy to find, and without stigma. It should be an inviting place where staff and students will not be interrupted throughout the day.

6. Educate parents. They need to know how the school will handle a crisis, why students may need a Safe Room, and who will work with them there. Integrate information into parent newsletters or other routine communications that are sent home early in the year. Remember that parents also relate best to those from their own culture, especially on sensitive issues that differ from their cultural norms.

Integrating Safe Rooms Into School Culture

Some administrators and teachers admit that their first experience with a Safe Room was less than they expected because many of the students who needed it chose to stay in class. It often takes a while before the appeal of a Safe Room is fully realized and appreciated. Students may have inhibitions or fears about what others will think if they stop by the Safe Room. They may also shy away if the Safe Room announcement is not delivered directly and without a shred of connotation, or if the Safe Room location has negative associations for students (such as being in a special education or speech pathology classroom). Ideally, of course, no room in which students receive assistance would carry negative connotations, but it is essential to remove any objections students may have toward using the Safe Room.

In other cases, teachers may resist encouraging their students to use the Safe Room because they feel it diminishes their own roles as primary caregivers. Students in need of support or advice often seek out teachers after school or at times when others are not around. This kind of fostering relationship between student and teacher reinforces the feeling that their connection is out of the ordinary. No one can take the place of a much beloved and respected teacher. Any initial resistance usually passes once teachers see the true value of the Safe Room.

In the beginning of a crisis, students simply need to know that staff has set aside a special place for them. This sends the priceless message that the adults in their world care for them. As the day progresses, some students will begin to use the room, and more will join in. It is preferable to send students the message that the school is willing—so far as possible—to let them select the time and place where their emotional needs can be met. Integrating the Safe Room concept into the school's crisis response plan and culture may take several trial runs—but ultimately, the Safe Room is a process, not an event.

A Strong Foundation

The rest of the book provides many details, ideas, and skill-building strategies for creating an effective Safe Room. The next chapter will discuss the process of establishing and running a Safe Room, including setting up and staffing the Safe Room, announcing the Safe Room to students, referring students to and dismissing them from the Safe Room, tracking Safe Room attendance, managing behavior in the Safe Room, debriefing Safe Room staff, and other practical aspects.

Chapter 3 will discuss grief and trauma and how they manifest in students at different ages. Signs that a student may need professional referral are also included. Chapter 4 will give examples of training exercises that help staff and students understand and process grief and trauma, and chapter 5 will explore some typical Safe Room conversations and describe how Safe Room staff can best respond to grieving students. Chapter 6 will cover a range of appropriate Safe Room activities for children and youth processing loss, and chapter 7 will close with a discussion of unique and difficult circumstances that require special measures.

Operating a Safe Room may seem to be especially challenging or to require a particular level of sophistication. For the most part, it requires a good protocol, plenty of supplies, enough space, the right environment, and well-trained staff. If the Safe Room works well and students use it, the closure of the mourning phase can be natural, healthy, and timely.

Laying a solid foundation for the Safe Room will produce the best experience for students and staff. Do not wait for the "really big" crisis to set up your first Safe Room. Plan now for how the Safe Room will be structured and run. Then you will be ready to use it for every loss and will have time to refine your procedures before your school community suffers a truly catastrophic event.

Chapter 2

The Safe Room Process

Chapter Overview

Sections

Checklists and Handouts

• • • • • • • • • • • • • • • •

The Safe Room is the heart of your crisis response. A Safe Room works well when local school administrators support the basic concept, when there is adequate planning, when the skill level of those who participate in the planning and implementation of Safe Rooms is high, and when the staff-to-student ratio in the Safe Room is adequately proportionate.

Although Safe Rooms greatly benefit students in the aftermath of a crisis, they also tend to make administrators uncomfortable. Student behavior in a Safe Room that does not have a sound foundation can escalate out of control and add to the crisis. This gives added importance to taking care with each step of implementation, from creating a clear and concise Safe Room announcement to managing student behavior in the Safe Room and determining when and how to send students back to their classrooms. ~

Creating the Safe Room

Open your Safe Room as soon as possible after a critical event. The number of days that a Safe Room will be open should be determined by student need. By the end of the first day, Safe Room staff will usually have an idea of how many students might need to return to the Safe Room the next day. By the second day, only half as many Safe Room staff members may be needed, and the Safe Room may be operated in a smaller room. By the third day, students might visit the counselor instead of the Safe Room—or one Safe Room staff member might have lunch with a small group of particularly affected students. The Safe Room should also reopen for a few hours after the funeral or school memory event (often held on the morning of the funeral, or, if the funeral will be held over the weekend, on a

Friday). After a catastrophic event such a school shooting, the Safe Room may need to be open for many more days.

A variety of rooms might be suitable for conversion into a Safe Room, such as the school library, media center, or an empty classroom. The room should be private, easy to find, comfortable, and without any stigma or negative associations for students. It should have tables for group work and spaces for private, one-to-one conversations. Telephone access is also important. You may need to rearrange the room to create a more welcoming atmosphere or to create discrete areas. Make it easy to monitor student access to the room, both to provide privacy and to prevent students from wandering in and out.

Ideally, a Safe Room should not serve a dual purpose, but if it is unavoidable, always consider who will be displaced by the Safe Room and what activities will change. Using a library, for example, may mean that students will check out books or return materials, walking in and out of the room while others are trying to process their grief. Many schools simply announce that the library will be closed for a number of days. If an entire room cannot be dedicated to the Safe Room, create discrete areas for Safe Room visitors and for the room's regular users, and use nametags to identify those who have checked in to work on their grief. Be certain that neither party's activities will disrupt the other's, and make sure that student privacy and confidentiality can be maintained.

If the Safe Room displaces a staff member who regularly uses that room during the day, consider including that person in the Safe Room training and process. Always return the room to its original condition and configuration at the end of each day.

After the Safe Room closes permanently, send a thank-you note to the person whose space was "appropriated."

Collect supplies for staff information, healthy refreshments, and activities ahead of time. Find a place to store them where the Rapid Response and Flight Team members can easily access them on crisis day (see the Safe Room Supplies Checklist, page 35).

Staffing the Safe Room

The previous chapter mentioned that a staff from outside the affected school, the Flight Team, should run the Safe Room. The Flight Team allows the rest of the building to remain stable, with familiar faces in familiar positions. Some districts may expect the support for students to come from within the building and will ask the school guidance counselor to operate the Safe Room. But the school counselor should remain in his or her own office. The Safe Room staff will need to send disruptive troubled students to the counselor for one-to-one support. Safe Room staff will also need to accompany students who disclose information that will have legal ramifications to the counselor's office—not only to ensure that school procedures for reporting and referral are followed, but also to establish a long-term on-site supportive relationship for those students.

Using a Flight Team to cover the extra tasks that arise ensures that you will have adequate staff during a critical time. You will need trained and experienced staff to set up the Safe Room, manage student behavior, call parents, make emergency referrals, and so on. After the initial crisis has passed and the Safe Room closes, the Flight Team will leave, and the school will have to manage the long-term effects of the crisis. That task is daunting enough; let others assist in the short term.

Most of the Safe Room staff members should be Flight Team members from outside the school; they are usually counselors, teachers, nurses, school psychologists, bilingual aides, or others who have had comprehensive training in children's grief, school crisis, trauma, and other dimensions of crisis response. However, it is helpful to have one or two local staff members in the Safe Room. Often this local representative may be a paraprofessional, librarian, or assistant librarian. Remember, your Safe Room staff's diversity should reflect the cultural and ethnic backgrounds of students who will be using the Safe Room.

While the Flight Team is in place, all parties must be aware that the principal of the building is in charge of all activities, including the Safe Room. Be certain that he or she is aware and approves of what the Safe Room will provide and how it will be managed.

The Safe Room staff is composed of a Safe Room coordinator and the number of staff members needed to maintain an adequate staff-to-student ratio. One-to-eight is terrific; one-to-ten works well. It is possible to manage behavior with far less, but much depends on the type of loss, the age of the students, and other factors.

The **Safe Room coordinator** serves as the lead person in the Safe Room (see the Safe Room Coordinator Checklist, page 37). He or she ensures that the Safe Room runs smoothly, from setting up the physical space to briefing Safe Room staff, monitoring staff-to-student ratios, keeping records of proceedings, and so on.

The coordinator also serves as a clearinghouse for all requests to the host school for supplies and information. It is important not to overwhelm school staff in a crisis with multiple requests from various members of the Safe Room team.

The coordinator needs to have a big-picture view of what is happening in the Safe Room, and for that reason he or she should not be responsible for directly supporting grieving children on a full-time basis. If more than one Safe Room is in use, the coordinator will need to move between them. Having one person in charge of all the Safe Rooms makes it easier to adjust the staffing and process as needed. For example, a coordinator could discover that one Safe Room has 20 students and another 60, even though both have the same number of staff members. The Safe Room coordinator can then shift students or team members to balance the staff-to-student ratio.

Safe Room staff work directly with children by helping them sign in and out, assessing their needs, monitoring group work, managing general behavior, talking one-to-one with particularly troubled children, keeping a record of those who may need professional referrals, and helping students decide when they are ready to return to class (see Safe Room Team Supplies Checklist, page 38).

At least a few Safe Room team members need to be adept at working with students who disclose intentions of suicide. Determine ahead of time:

- Who will decide the need for a suicide assessment
- What kind of assessment will be used

- Who will conduct the assessment

- To whom formal referrals will be made

- Who will do the record-keeping for the school or district

- Who will keep the paper trail for the Flight Team's verification of formal written referrals (usually the Safe Room coordinator)

Finally, Safe Room staff also need to provide relief for each other. In a crisis, we often work so hard to meet the needs of students that our own energy becomes depleted. Staff members can avoid this problem by taking breaks, asking for help when they need it, and offering help when they see another staff member needs it. In doing so, they will take care of themselves *and* model good self-care.

Making the Announcement

When it is necessary to inform students about a death or crisis in the school community, it is preferable for each teacher to make the announcement in his or her classroom rather than for the principal to call a student assembly or read the announcement over the public address system. The teacher has a better sense of when to make the announcement and can more easily prepare students for bad news and guide them into a discussion afterwards. Additionally, the teacher is better able to notice students whose adverse reactions may indicate their need for the Safe Room or for professional support. In an assembly setting, those who leave in tears or are badly shaken by the news can quickly disappear unnoticed behind bleachers or into the bathrooms. Some are too embarrassed to ask for help. Many are overlooked.

A Dual Obligation: Confidentiality and Disclosure

Although a nondisclosure statement is not legally binding, it is helpful to have all Safe Room staff and Flight Team members sign one (see page 39 for a reproducible nondisclosure statement). This document can serve as a record of all adults who staffed the Safe Room during the crisis, and it reminds everyone that the staff's primary function is to support students. Confidentiality of student disclosure is crucial, but Safe Room team members are also under a professional and ethical obligation to report any knowledge of students who are in danger of hurting themselves or others, students who are victims of child abuse or sexual abuse, and any other incidents that must be brought to the attention of school personnel or authorities. Have the means and protocol clearly established to handle any of these circumstances before a situation arises in a Safe Room.

All teachers should make the announcement during the same period to prevent students from learning the news in the hallways between classes. Remember that teachers will need a moment to respond to the announcement themselves. Use "runners" to distribute the announcements, and be sure they ask teachers to step outside the classroom to receive the news.

Guidelines for Announcing a Death or Tragedy

When making the announcement, teachers should take the following steps:

1. Get students' attention, ask them to sit down, and warn them that you have bad news.

2. Read the details of the bad news, and give funeral information, if it is available. It works best for each teacher to read the statement and any other necessary administrative memos concerning the event carefully, *as written* by the principal or administrator. Stick to the facts.

3. **Normalize student reactions.** Note that those who were close to the deceased student may be very affected, while others may be less affected. "Normalizing" is the process of letting someone know that others have had similar reactions through statements such as, "I've heard others say the same kind of thing," or, "It isn't uncommon for students to feel that way."

4. **Announce that the library (or another room) is open for students to gather.** *Do not use the words "Safe Room"* as this may turn students away. The announcement should never refer to "the Safe Room," "the Counseling Center," or other terms that suggest special need. It is important that students do not think of the Safe Room as a place "for kids" and then avoid coming because of that perception. Call the Safe Room by a neutral name such as "the drop-in center," or simply say, "The library won't be available for regular use today because we're making the space available for students who want to gather together."

5. **Open a discussion.** After reading the announcement, begin by asking who knew the student, who has experienced a death before, and so on. The discussion held in each classroom following the announcement is especially important (see chapter 7, page 141, for more details on directing this discussion under unique and difficult circumstances). It gives the teacher a chance to stop the rumor mill by making direct comments and announcements. When students have clear information, they are less prone to speculate. Being forthright will alleviate fears, suspicions, and stress for everyone.

6. Encourage students to respect each other's feelings. Discussion creates a teachable moment that can do more than help grieving students—it can teach all students empathy and compassion. Integrating these kinds of discussions into the school day gradually changes the school environment as students gain a language of compassion. They begin to realize the importance of telling what they know, of taking responsibility for letting adults know when students are at risk or when they might be thinking of putting others at risk, and of respecting those who are different from them and their friends. This is the foundation of listening to those who are grieving, of comforting them, and of giving meaning to death.

7. Suggest that anyone who wants to go to the library can sign out of class. Let students know that they will be required to sign out of class and sign in to the Safe Room when they arrive.

The "room with the empty desk"—the classroom of the missing or deceased student—will be particularly affected by the loss. Often the classroom with the empty desk operates very much like a Safe Room all day long. A Flight Team member can be stationed there to guide an activity for the whole class and to watch for students who need to go to the Safe Room. Flight Team members should travel through the school during the day to visit all of the student's other classrooms.

Keeping Students at School

Encourage grieving students to stay at school. By staying in school and, as needed, in the Safe Room, they will learn new coping skills. Remember, grief is processed best in the environment of the loss. Students who miss the first few days of grieving with their peers often have more difficulty later. (The exception to this is those who have significant issues unrelated to the school loss and have nothing in common with grieving peers, such as a student who is terminally ill and really does need parental support or reassurance from a physician.) Once the other students have moved on from their mourning, there is no way to recreate the shared grief process for the students who went home.

Tell students they can choose to be in the Safe Room, in their classrooms, or in other areas supervised by an adult. If they ask to go home, ask if a phone call to a parent might help them make it through the day. Having a parent come to the school to be with the child for a while may also work. If a child wants to talk with a parent, be sure to call the parent yourself first. Explain the situation, describe the wonderful support the school is providing, and educate the parent on the importance of grieving in the environment of the loss. Help the parent understand that encouraging his or her child to stay at school will help the child cope with the loss better.

If these strategies do not work, follow school procedures for allowing students to check out of school. Be aware that the procedures for checking students out of school on crisis days may be more detailed and require more information than on ordinary days, depending on the nature of the event.

Referring Students to the Safe Room

After hearing the announcement and discussing the death in the classroom, many students will be ready to return to academics. However, for those students who either knew the deceased

Teachers as Gatekeepers

Because the stakes are high and the signs of need can be difficult to read, it is recommended that teachers release any student who wishes to access the Safe Room. Teachers may be tempted to keep students who "don't really need" to go to the Safe Room in class, but they should avoid becoming gatekeepers. Safe Room team members are better trained to determine each student's level of need, and since Safe Room staff have no teaching duties, they can focus on those most affected by the event. Teachers can be of greater service to less affected students—by focusing on teaching.

Gatekeeping can have serious consequences. It increases the likelihood that suicidal students will go unidentified and move closer to the edge. For many suicidal students, it may be easier to disclose suicidal thoughts in a Safe Room than in the classroom. Safe Room staff will be equipped to recognize these students, alert the school, and ensure that someone from the school follows the procedure for referring the student to an appropriate level of therapy or in-patient care.

or have some other unresolved loss, the classroom discussion will not be enough, and their grief often makes them disruptive. The Safe Room exists for these students who are unable to learn until they can work through a large piece of their grief. The Safe Room gives them a place to go to focus on their grief, allowing less affected students to continue their academic studies. The grieving students will return to the classroom when they are once again ready to learn.

In some cases, depending on the age of the students, schools implement a buddy system in which a peer accompanies students to the Safe Room. These kinds of arrangements can be determined either at the building level or on a case-by-case basis, depending on teacher judgment or the student's desire.

Teachers and other school staff need to know that the Safe Room staff has the ability to give genuinely skilled care. They also need assurance that students using the Safe Room to dodge class will be quickly identified and sent back to class. If the Safe Room is staffed well enough, it is possible to give even those who come to dawdle or gawk a short lesson on empathy and compassion.

Admitting Students to the Safe Room

Have a process for students to sign out of their classrooms and into the Safe Room. (See the Drop-In Center Sign-In/Sign-Out Sheet, page 41.) This sends the message that this is not an opportunity to skip class for a cigarette, leave campus, or hang out in the bathrooms. Although it is unnecessary to reconcile the times between classrooms and the Safe Room, signing in and out encourages students to move more directly from the classroom to the Safe Room without side trips.

Welcome and Engage

Once students arrive at the Safe Room, an adult should welcome them and direct them to sign in. At the sign-in area, another staff member should go over the rules of the Safe Room. Rules should be few and broad in scope, such as "Students will be respectful in all ways. Students will behave responsibly." Post these rules so that all students know them. In addition, make it clear to all students that everyone is expected to work on an activity; have a variety of activities available with all the necessary supplies. Although students are allowed to talk with each other about their feelings and memories, the expectation of group or individual activity will give Safe Room staff something to fall back on when they need students to be focused and quiet. Students should also be reminded that what other students say is private and should not be repeated outside the Safe Room.

Identify and Refer High Risk Students

It is critical that Safe Room staff be prepared to assess students' needs. After a tragedy, in both the Safe Room and in the school as a whole, students and adults will exhibit different expressions of grief. One group may be in shock, denial, or confusion. This group will probably include those who knew the deceased personally and are at the initial stage of the grief process. Another group might be in a more full-blown, open state of grief and may be crying or sobbing. These students may or may not have known the deceased. Some of those who are sobbing and crying and *did not personally know the deceased* could be incredibly distraught because they are dealing with an unresolved death in their past. The current tragedy may have broken down their defenses and returned them to the pain of an earlier time. Others might be displaying amplified emotions *because* the school-related loss was a friend. See chapter 5, pages 85–89, for more information on assessing student needs.

In respecting the different needs of students that may show up at the Safe Room, it is sometimes helpful to encourage them to gather by type of loss. Each table in the Safe Room can, theoretically, have a different focus. For example, having a whole table of students who have lost grandparents creates a mini-support group for them. Because of the bonds they make on such a day, these students sometimes seek each other out long after the Safe Room is no longer in operation. In fact, Safe Room staff can identify students with similar losses who might benefit from a grief support group to be offered by the school counselor on an ongoing basis, if desired.

A small number of students may have a very high need to grieve privately. These students would benefit from one-to-one work with the school counselor or time alone. Safe Room staff must be sensitive to the varying styles and needs of these children. Chapter 5 (page 85) will address this aspect of the process in more detail.

Managing Behavior in the Safe Room

Perhaps more than any other element, effective behavior management in the Safe Room is of paramount importance. The school administration may not approve a Safe Room *next* time if behavior gets out of control *this time.* Everyone working in the Safe Room must be comfortable intervening with the whole group to manage behavior, state rules, offer activities, restrict distractions, and enforce the rules—with a gentle hand.

The foundation for optimum behavior in the Safe Room is clearly stating the rules when students arrive and offering a variety of activities that students must choose from (see chapter 6, page 111). Students should be permitted to stay in the Safe Room only as long as they are really working on processing their grief. Safe Room staff should make it clear that students are expected to "plug in" to a meaningful activity or some other means of working on grief or trauma.

It must also be clear that the Safe Room is not a place to "kick back" or play video games or chess. There must be restrictions for items such as cell phones, pagers, handheld gaming systems, and laptops. Computer use can be tricky. In one case, following the death of a middle-school boy, several students in the Safe Room wanted to use the computers to make posters to put up around the school. They arranged a few scanned pictures and included the student's name, birth date, death date, and a few words that described their classmate and how they would miss him. Although this seemed like a reasonable use of the computers, it was not long before students were playing computer games and surfing the Net. It is not necessary to create a rule that no one can ever use a computer in the Safe Room, but think ahead about who will monitor activities, and how—and have a plan in case a similar circumstance arises.

Noise and other behavioral issues can also come up and should be dealt with promptly. If students are being too noisy, walk over to the light switch, flip it on and off a couple of times, and ask, "Somebody tell me. What is the drop-in center for?" Often some smart-mouthed student is apt to say, "To get out of history!" Take that opportunity to validate that although many students probably think about using the drop-in center as a place to get out of a class, it really is for students who are grieving. Announce that this a good time for those who are not grieving to sign out of the drop-in center and head back to class. If a student appears to be disruptive for emotional rather than behavioral issues, that student should be taken to the school counselor for one-to-one work.

It is easy for behaviors in the Safe Room to escalate. Having well-trained Safe Room staff helps identify those students who are not there for processing, sharing memories, planning the memory event, or other appropriate activities. Being clear, being assertive, remaining kind, and remaining open almost always works.

Returning Students to Class

The length of stay in the Safe Room is determined by each student's individual needs. Many will actively grieve for a half hour or an hour, and will then be ready to return to class. Those students who knew the deceased or have particularly painful experiences in their personal lives may be in the Safe Room for much of the day. This is usually a minority, but there are no rules about time limits.

It is crucial that the Safe Room staff send students back to class once they are ready. Students will grieve the loss over time and in spurts. Some will be in and out of the Safe Room more than once in a day. Some will not finish their grief in their Safe Room visits, and some will have follow-up needs as well.

Again, be assertive in helping students make the decision to return to class if they have finished the most immediate part of their grief work and appear ready. For instance, after completing several activities, a group of students who earlier were talking appropriately may start talking more boisterously and laughing about other topics. A Safe Room staff member might go over and kindly and clearly make a statement of observation:

"I'm noticing that while you were working on your cards for the family, you were all really focused on Jenny's life and your memories and her death. Now your conversation sounds like you're ready for a break from that. How about you go back to your classroom now? If you need to drop back in later, we'll be here."

Be sure to have a quick, informal conversation with those students who leave the Safe Room to make sure they are okay. Tell them it is perfectly acceptable for them to return later if they desire. Ask questions to help the student prepare for handling his or her grief outside of the Safe Room:

- "What's going to happen when you get home tonight?"

- "Will your family support be different than the support at school today?"

- "Who can you call if you feel sad?"

- "If you wake up at night and feel scared, could you wake your parents?" [Encourage students to ask parents this.]

- "Is there anything we could do to help that we haven't thought of yet?"

Sometimes students appear to be ready to go back to their classrooms, but seem reluctant to leave the Safe Room. It is a good idea to have tickets made ahead of time—similar to popular board-game cards—saying "Free Ticket Back" so students can know they will be welcome if they need to return to the Safe Room. Often just having this ticket as a reminder is all they will need.

Debriefing Safe Room Staff

Students are not the only ones who need to express their feelings and reactions to a crisis; Safe Room team members also need time to "de-stress" through debriefings at the end of each day and at the end of the crisis response as a whole.

The Debriefing Controversy

Debriefings are intentional gatherings of those who experienced a potentially traumatizing event. The group is guided through a discussion in a way that helps reduce their risk of psychological trauma by helping them verbalize their reactions and responses to the event. A debriefing or other intervention is essential for people who suffer impact from traumatic events because it helps restore a sense of balance and health.

The effectiveness of debriefing has been the subject of some controversy in recent years, in part due to misapplication of certain techniques. Jeffrey Mitchell first created what he called Critical Incident Stress Debriefing (CISD) in 1983. It was a technique designed specifically for emergency responders exposed to traumatic events, but CISD (sometimes called CISM, Critical Incident Stress Management) has been indiscriminately applied to many other populations as well—populations with entirely different needs, for whom it was never intended.

Emergency responders, for example, arrive on the scene after a crisis has already occurred. They have uniforms, training, skills, back-up support, and a specific role to perform on the scene. When their work is done, they are free to leave. After a traumatic event, an emergency responder wonders, "Did I do a good job?"

In contrast, victims have been caught completely by surprise—and surprise is a significant indicator of the potential for trauma (see chapter 3, page 55, for more on trauma). Victims are usually not prepared with crisis training, and they are often unsure what role, if any, they play as events unfold. If the victim is a child, he or she may not be at a developmental stage to understand what has happened or what the consequences will be. After a traumatic event, a victim asks, "Is the world a safe place?"

Clearly, a victim's needs require a more specialized, flexible approach. This resource does not suggest that Safe Room staff should debrief traumatized children. The Safe Room provides a short-term intervention; Safe Room staff use gentle, informal questioning to identify those children who may need long-term assistance. They then ensure that at-risk students are referred to a trained mental health professional for assessment and possible clinical diagnosis.

Safe Room staff, however, may still benefit from an informal debriefing at the end of each response day. The debriefing for Safe room staff is much less formal than for victims, bystanders, or emergency workers who were on the scene. Safe Room staff are highly unlikely to be traumatized. They have not had to mobilize the fight-or-flight response in order to survive the day. They have warning that they are going into the situation, so they are not surprised, unlike victims or bystanders. They have training, back-up, and a specific role, but unlike emergency responders, Safe Room staff are not dealing with critical matters of life and death. By the time a Safe Room is established, the highly charged moments of the crisis are over.

No one is brandishing a weapon. No one needs immediate medical attention. No one is dying.

Safe Room staff have, however, heard painful stories and witnessed strong emotions. Their work is exhausting and apt to create persistent feelings and reactions. Often the return to "normal life" requires some talking with others to give meaning to the experience and integrate that meaning into their lives. An informal debriefing offers Safe Room staff an opportunity to reflect on the day, to voice concerns or issues, and to decompress before going home—in a manner that preserves student confidentiality.

Crisis Day Debriefing

At the end of the first day of the crisis, the debriefing should include the Rapid Response team members, the Flight Team leader, and any Flight Team members who provided support to parents or staff elsewhere in the school, such as in the classroom with the empty desk.

This is also a time to identify those students who may have been traumatized, who have disclosed serious personal issues, or who may be at risk for suicide. Safe Room staff may know of students who have not been previously identified as at risk by school staff. These students will need special care to help them recover from the event and to prevent another crisis. Refer them to the school counselor, and be sure they receive adequate care and follow-up until they are no longer at risk.

At the close of the initial debriefing, remind the Flight Team of the importance of confidentiality. When people respond to the needs of another site, the staff in their own buildings will often ask how the response went when the team members return. It is easy for team members to say more than is appropriate, especially because the people asking are usually doing so out of genuine concern and caring.

It is best if a Flight Team member who was not on campus during the event can lead the debriefing. The person leading the debriefing needs to have training in intervention, but does not need to be from an outside organization. Sometimes the team leader leads the debriefing, but care should be taken to ensure that this person also has someone who will soon provide the same support for him or her as well. See page 42 for a list of Safe Room staff debriefing questions. Give every Safe Room staff member a copy of the handout "Ways to Take Care of Yourself at Times of Loss" from page 108.

Hold additional debriefings at the end of every day that the Safe Room remains open.

Safe Room Follow-Up Debriefing

A week or so after the crisis response, the entire response team should meet for a follow-up debriefing to support team members who worked the response, to evaluate the response, and to improve the crisis response plan. A follow-up meeting helps everyone recover and learn from the experience. See page 43 for a sample agenda of a follow-up debriefing.

1. Recap event details. Cover the basic facts of the crisis, the response efforts of the team, and allow team members to review their experience as a group.

2. Address lingering issues. Individual members can talk about aspects of the response that have continued to haunt them or that they have not been able to let go. This can be helpful in the recovery process for everyone.

3. Offer staff support. This can be a good time to offer a list of internal and external resources for staff members who may need further help in processing what they have experienced while responding to the crisis or helping students in the Safe Room.

4. Identify areas for improvement. This debriefing is also a great time for the crisis response staff to identify what went well and what lessons were learned. Keep the discussion open to everyone, and be sure that someone takes careful notes for the district and the Flight Team to incorporate into their plans. This information can be invaluable when the next crisis strikes. Disseminate these notes to the whole Flight Team, not just those members who responded to this event.

Evaluating the Safe Room

It is always important to evaluate how well the Safe Room operated and what challenges occurred. This will bring a sense of closure to each event in terms of the team's involvement, and it provides the information needed to continually improve responses. Something that does not go well can continue to trouble team members until the team engages in some problem-solving and makes a change to ensure the difficulty will not happen again, or in the same way, to someone else.

Approach this meeting as an opportunity to gather suggestions from staff that will identify any weaknesses within the current Safe Room plan. The purpose is not to judge, but to provide helpful information for the next crisis. It is fair to assume that all who volunteer and train to be in the Safe Room are doing their very best to meet student or staff needs. Pointing fingers or assigning blame for mistakes or problems that arose will undermine future response efforts and the team's morale.

Thoroughly and objectively evaluating the Safe Room process after each situation will bring relief similar to the relief experienced after a debriefing. The reproducible Safe Room evaluation on page 45 will help in this process.

Safe Room Supplies Checklist

There is no specific mix of supplies for the Safe Room. The goal is to provide a variety of ways for students to process their grief and anguish. Activities depend on available supplies, and activities provide the structure for learning and for managing behavior. A sampling of some possible Safe Room items follows.

Signs and Identification

__ A sign listing Safe Room rules

__ Signs for the hallway directing students to the location of the Safe Room

__ Sign-in and sign-out sheet (see page 41)

__ Nametags for staff (the people running the Safe Room might not be known to students)

__ Nametags for students (optional)

Information

__ A copy of the announcement read in class

__ Fact sheet with information about the tragedy

__ Newspaper coverage, if appropriate (screen carefully)

__ List of community resources

__ Handouts on self-care for students, staff, and Safe Room staff

__ Confidential folder (Place this folder in a location inaccessible to students and include in it information on the crisis event that would be helpful to staff, such as the nondisclosure statement, a list of students who might be particularly at risk, newspaper clippings that contain graphic or explicit detail, information about staff meetings, and so on.)

Environment and Items for the Safe Room

___ Private, individual space for students who want to be alone

___ Telephone

___ Chairs and tables

___ Paper, pens, tape, scissors, and items for writing and drawing and creating signs

___ Facial tissue

___ Books and other grief-related resource materials that are age-appropriate and carefully selected

___ Tape or CD player and a selection of relaxing music

___ Stuffed animals, big pillows, blankets, "comfy" things

___ Activities and supplies (see chapter 6, page 111)

Refreshments and Accessory Items

Avoid any items with high sugar content and low nutritional value, such as cookies and carbonated drinks.

___ Food (fruit, cheese, crackers, or cinnamon toast supplies—even though it has a small amount of sugar sprinkled on top, cinnamon toast has a great welcoming aroma)

___ Drinks (fruit juices, water, unsweetened tea, and so on)

___ Paper plates, napkins, any utensils needed

___ Toaster

___ Cooler or mini-fridge

The Safe Room • Copyright © 2006 by Cheri Lovre
Solution Tree • www.solution-tree.com

Safe Room Coordinator Checklist

• • • • • • • • • • • • • • • •

The number and kinds of Safe Rooms that are needed will depend on each unique situation and are best determined on a case-by-case basis. The Safe Room coordinator has the following responsibilities:

___ Attend all Flight Team meetings.

___ Set up Safe Rooms.

___ Monitor supplies and the staff-to-student or adult-to-student ratio in each Safe Room.

___ Keep lines of communication open with administrators.

___ Keep track of the Safe Room staff.

___ Coordinate requests for supplies and information, and make sure they are filled.

___ Keep the paper trail for the Flight Team verification of formal written referrals.

___ Keep records and create the paper trail for the school or district.

___ Explain and uphold the policy of not admitting parents to those who want to enter the student Safe Room.

___ Lead debriefings or locate a Flight Team member who can lead them.

___ Ensure that all Safe Room staff members attend debriefings.

___ Refer Safe Room staff for professional help as needed.

___ Collect information on how the Safe Room operated, and summarize and distribute any findings that could be helpful for the next Safe Room.

Safe Room Team Supplies Checklist

• • • • • • • • • • • • • • • • • •

Each team member should receive a three-ring tabbed binder containing:

__ A single map clearly showing the location of each school in the county (in case team members need to travel between schools—for large counties, these maps can just show location from the nearest highway or well-known street)

__ A mini–floor plan of each building (8½ x 11 sheet of paper) that identifies:

  __ The location of the Safe Room

  __ The locations of the restrooms, staff lounge, front office, and other important locations

__ A schedule of the bells that indicate lunch, recess, and break times

__ Phone extension numbers for key individuals at each building, particularly the administrators, counselors, nurses, and the person whose room is designated to be used as the Safe Room

__ Clear directions on how to use the phones

__ Legal policies and school policies that are relevant to crises

__ Information on the LOVRE model (page 93)

__ Resource material

  __ Flight Team Nondisclosure Statement (page 39)

  __ Signs That a Student May Need Professional Help (page 65)

  __ Safe Room Evaluation (page 45)

Flight Team Nondisclosure Statement

The members of the Flight Team affirm their belief in the worth and dignity of the individual and believe that it is their professional responsibility to fully respect the right to privacy of staff and students involved in Flight Team responses. What occurs in the Safe Room is confidential.

Confidentiality of personally identifiable information includes, but is not limited to:

- Student and staff names

- Names of the student and staff members' family

- Any information that would reveal the student or staff member's identity, such as addresses and Social Security numbers

Confidentiality will not be abridged by the Flight Team member except:

- Where there is a clear and present danger to the student, staff or other persons

- When it is in the interest of the student or staff member to consult with others (such as the school principal, designated team leader, Flight Team coordinator, ESD supervisor, mental health supervisor).

- When the student or staff member waives this right in writing (This could happen if the coroner asks if some students have information that could clarify something about the death. This would definitely be the exception, not the rule. Flight Team members work hard to focus their efforts on helping the students, not on assisting outside people or agencies.)

- During confidential Flight Team debriefings

When Flight Team members respond to a school's crisis call, they are acting in a volunteer role and are therefore required to follow that school's policies and procedures and defer to the decisions of the building administrator. *Flight Team members have the professional responsibility to be certain that all child abuse or other situations that require reporting are reported to the appropriate agency.*

Professional ethics and confidentiality are most important. Flight Team volunteers are expected to comply with all of the district's rules and regulations.

My signature below certifies that I have read, fully understand, and agree with the information above and agree to abide by these procedures. My signature also indicates that I understand that the good will of the Flight Team depends upon, among other things, keeping information confidential.

_____

Flight Team Member   Date

_____

Flight Team Member   Date

_____

Flight Team Member   Date

_____

Flight Team Member   Date

_____

Flight Team Member   Date

_____

Flight Team Member   Date

The Safe Room • Copyright © 2006 by Cheri Lovre
Solution Tree • www.solution-tree.com

Drop-In Center Sign-In/Sign-Out Sheet

· · · · · · · · · · · · · · · · · ·

School _____   Date _____

Name	Time In	Time Out
_____	_____	_____
_____	_____	_____
_____	_____	_____
_____	_____	_____
_____	_____	_____
_____	_____	_____
_____	_____	_____
_____	_____	_____
_____	_____	_____
_____	_____	_____
_____	_____	_____
_____	_____	_____
_____	_____	_____
_____	_____	_____

Debriefing Questions for Safe Room Staff

Safe Room staff and other adults who give all of their energy to supporting students during a crisis will find that they may need considerable support themselves by the end of each day that they serve in a school. Not everyone needs to respond to every question listed here. Everyone does, however, need the opportunity to put words to the experience, to have others bear witness to their process, to be reminded of the importance of confidentiality, and to shift toward a more relaxed state before leaving the school. Some key questions are:

- What happened as you provided the Safe Room response today?

- What were some of your reactions during the day?

- What are you feeling right now?

- Are there parts that are lingering for you?

- Were there things that students said or asked that were particularly difficult?

- Are there students who may require further counseling or who appear to be at risk for suicide or trauma or for other reasons?

- What worked well?

- What could be improved?

- How could you have felt more supported during the day?

- How could you be supported right now?

- What changes could we make in the crisis response plan based on your experience?

- What are you going to do to take really good care of yourself tonight?

Sample Agenda for Follow-Up Debriefing

• • • • • • • • • • • • • • • • •

All Safe Room staff must have a chance to find closure to the crisis through a follow-up meeting. This meeting will allow staff and other Flight Team members who participated in the process to address any unresolved issues, evaluate and improve the process, and identify those students who need additional support.

1. Begin by stating your appreciation for the staff's efforts and reminding all of the purpose—to give those who participated in the response one more time to diffuse the lingering energy they hold, to find support from the larger group, and to identify lessons learned and improvements to be made to the plan.

2. Briefly describe the event and circumstances.

3. Ask each Safe Room staff member to describe his or her participation and experience:

   • What he or she did

   • How the day(s) went

   • Anything about his or her experience that is still lingering

4. Invite Flight Team members to discuss what could have been handled better and suggestions for improving the response plan or protocols. Some questions to address:

   • What worked well?

   • What could be improved?

   • How could you have felt more supported during the day?

   • What changes could we make in the Safe Room plan or crisis response plan based on your experience?

5. Open it up for any team members to comment.

6. Be sure to praise those who provided services to the school in need.

7. Collect all suggestions and distribute a written list of them to everyone associated with the team.

8. End with informal social time.

Safe Room Evaluation

● ● ● ● ● ● ● ● ● ● ● ● ● ● ● ● ● ● ●

School _____   Date _____

(To be filled out by Flight Team members who staff the Safe Room or who respond to a school site.)

Name _____   School _____

Your assignment or role _____   Date _____

What worked well?

_____

_____

_____

_____

_____

_____

_____

_____

_____

What could be improved?

_____

_____

_____

_____

_____

_____

_____

_____

_____

_____

What about the room arrangement or environment was particularly helpful or could have been better structured another time?

_____
_____
_____
_____
_____
_____
_____
_____
_____

What was done for the staff person who gave up his or her space for the Safe Room? Did you provide extra debriefing, leave a special note behind, or send a card of appreciation?

_____
_____
_____
_____
_____
_____
_____
_____
_____

What suggestions do you have for future Safe Rooms? Do you have other comments?

_____
_____
_____
_____
_____
_____
_____
_____
_____

Chapter 3

Understanding
Grief and Trauma

GRIEF AND
TRAUMA

• • • • • • • • • • • • • • • •

It is essential that Safe Room staff understand the difference between trauma and grief. Many of us are not adept at differentiating trauma from grief, however. Not only does the average person not understand the difference, many counselors and therapists have no clear understanding of it, either. This can result in victims receiving therapy that does not meet their unique needs. Safe Room approaches must vary according to the nature of the student's response as well as his or her developmental stage in understanding and processing loss.

Grief

Since most counselors and adults are familiar with grief, a brief summary may suffice to contrast it with trauma, which is the main focus of this chapter. Grief is an emotional, heart-centered response to the loss of something loved. Grief is characterized by sadness, anger, guilt, and other emotions. It may temporarily diminish our cognitive abilities and stress our physical well-being: We may suffer headaches, abdominal troubles, or other physical reactions. Although people who were close to the deceased will continue grieving at their own pace, often for years, the frequency and duration of periods of grief usually drop considerably over time.

Grief is processed both socially and internally. The communal aspect of grief is mourning. We mourn through rituals and traditions at social gatherings like funerals, memorial services, and wakes. A funeral meets the family's needs for this kind of publicly shared grief; a school memory event meets the students' needs and marks the end of the school's formal period of grieving. Mourning might be most evident between the time of the death and the school memory event.

We also process grief internally. This private aspect of grief occurs whether or not we have the opportunity to mourn in community. Even if a school chooses not to have a Safe Room or a memory event, students who knew and loved the deceased will struggle with grief. In fact, without the support and validation that mourning provides, the grieving process will likely be more complicated and last longer for those students most affected by the death.

The Tasks of Grief

Alan Wolfelt (1983, 1992, 1997) has written extensively on grief, particularly on children in grief. There are many wonderful authors who now have provided much insight in this field, but his conception of the "tasks of grief" is succinct and pertinent for Safe Room staff.

Like adults, Wolfelt suggests, children need compassion and support to pass through specific steps or "tasks" that help them process grief. These can be translated into tasks for their adult caregivers. The steps on pages 50–51 have been adapted from Wolfelt's conceptual framework for this application.

Grief is not a mental illness. It is the natural human reaction to the loss of someone loved. Some losses are never entirely reconciled. We lack even the language to express what happens to grief over time: Do we "recover," or do we merely "cope"? What we do know is that the frequency, duration, and intensity of grief changes. Years after someone we love dies, we may still cry—but not as often or for as long as we did in the first weeks after the death. The intensity of grief, however, can remain surprisingly potent. If we work at resolving or reconciling grief, we usually feel better over time—but we may also remain acutely aware of the power of the relationship and the depth of the loss, sometimes for the rest of our lives.

Supporting Children in Grief

1. Speak the truth. Children need to hear how the person died. Grief is dependent on the circumstances of the death: If our loved one dies of a brain aneurism, we have a different reaction than if the loved one was murdered. The quality of grief is determined by whether the death was "an act of God" or from human malice or negligence, by what we imagine our loved one went through, by whether we think he or she suffered, and so on. This is as true for children as it is for adults.

2. Help students express pain and sadness. Except for very young children, language plays a major role in processing grief. How the death is explained and how the child expresses his or her response will affect how well a child will cope with this and future losses. Putting words to grief and to the circumstances of the loss is often the first step in overcoming the usual initial reaction of denial. Encourage students to talk or otherwise express their emotional response to the death.

3. Encourage students to share memories. Sharing memories with others who also knew the deceased is the beginning of moving the relationship of life into one of memory. For this reason, it is crucial to create space for students to process grief at school rather than at home.

4. Help students explore how the death will change them personally. Often a death brings about a need to examine one's identity. For instance, if a student's only sibling dies, she might ask whether she is still a sister or has become an only child; over time, she will develop a new identity based on life without the deceased sibling.

(continued)

Supporting Children in Grief (continued)

5. **Give the death meaning.** Although the meaning we give a death may change over time, this important ongoing task is as critical in the early stages of grief as it is in the later stages. Children need adult support and guidance to interpret their experience of death in a healthy way. Unassisted children may infer meanings that are detrimental to the grieving process, such as "All people who go to the hospital die," or "If I had talked to my friend that night, she would not have committed suicide."

6. **Provide a way to say goodbye.** All cultures have some kind of ritual around death. Some have a wake or a celebration of life, while others have a more perfunctory ritual that centers on the disposal of the body. In Western cultures, the timing of the ritual often appears to bring closure to public mourning. After a funeral or wake, there is a certain sense of relief that the first step in saying goodbye has been taken, even though private grief may continue. Depending on the family and the culture, additional rituals and steps will occur over time.

7. **Provide ongoing support.** As we acknowledge that the grief may not be over for months or years, so, too, must we acknowledge the grievers' need for ongoing support. Schools need to be aware that students who lose close friends or family members will feel the impact for much longer than the first year.

GRIEF AND TRAUMA

The Developmental Stages of Understanding Death

In most cases, grieving people long for emotional connection. Often, just having loving companions on the journey of grief will be enough to comfort and heal. Being a good companion to students on the journey of grief requires a basic understanding of the developmental stages of understanding death.

The age of the child greatly affects his or her ability to understand death and process grief.

Due to individual differences in maturity and cognitive development, some children will be ahead of or behind others who are in their age group. Students will come to understand the reality of the death and loss at different rates. They will often be in denial at first, and adults may need to repeat the details of the event several times before students really grasp the finality of the loss. Using language that is appropriate to the child's developmental stage will help the child process grief. Support a child's capacity for grief, but do not try to push the child beyond his or her developmental stage. Though we might do it for "the right reasons" (because we care about them and think our wisdom will lessen their pain), it is usually counterproductive.

Under 3 (Preverbal)

At this stage, language skills are underdeveloped; children are unable to verbally express their feelings and reactions. Instead, they convey messages through their behavior and understand best those messages conveyed through others' behavior. Their greatest need is for comfort and immediate attention expressed physically through rocking, holding, nurturing, or singing lullabies at bedtime, preferably by a familiar person. If a parent has died, a consistent primary caregiver is crucial.

Ages 3–6 (Magical Thinking)

Children in this age group often believe they may have caused the death by magic or special powers. They frequently associate a death with concurrent places or events: If Grandma went to the hospital and died there, they may fear that other family members who go to the hospital will die, too. They need honest reassurance. Though Safe Room staff cannot promise that no one else will die, they can tell children, "It makes sense to me that you have that fear, but I don't expect this death to happen soon to anyone else we know."

Children in this age group display grief more sporadically than adults; they may cry for a while, then happily skip out to recess. They may be able to verbalize that someone has died, but only the repeated experience of missing that person day after day—an accumulated "gone-ness"—makes death real for them in an emotional sense. Often these younger children remember that Mommy has died only after weeks or even months of running downstairs for breakfast expecting to see her. For them, the feeling of her being gone grows over time until it finally becomes internalized and "real." As a result, it may appear that these children have delayed grief, but this apparent delay is a function of their inability to immediately understand what has happened.

Ages 6–9 (Concrete Reasoning)

Children at this age often create personifications of death: They may speak of the "death dropper" or the "angel of death." Around the age of 6, children often have great fascination with death and killing. They may want to stop in the parking lot to examine a squirrel that was hit by a car, for example. Near age 8, they might even have a morbid fascination with death rituals and also have dreams of death and resurrection (not only in Christian cultures but across all cultures and religions). They like to tell ghost stories and are superstitious, using oaths and chants to keep death and bad omens away. They may not understand or accept rational facts or adult observations about death.

At this stage, children talk about death in terms of non-movement or non-function by stating, for example, that the dead person cannot walk, talk, or move. They begin to conceptualize about losing a loved one and may suddenly realize the finality of death. This can bring about a great fear of losing their parents; they may repeatedly voice fears that their parents, or a parent, will die. They are moving away from magical thinking and toward grasping concepts of finality and irreversibility, but they continue to think of death as something that happens to others, not to themselves. They need concrete language: Refer to "death" and "died," not "passed away."

Ages 9–12 (Abstract Thinking)

By this time, youth have a more realistic understanding of death and may also be fascinated with the physiology of death. Some may want to view the body of the deceased. They may fixate on deaths that are sudden, violent, and unpredictable.

At this point in their lives, most youth have a sense of the universality of death. Some experience a fear of "the void" or imagine the spirit of a departed loved one in suspended animation—just hanging "out there" in the ether somewhere. Their broader understanding of death can also include a pervasive fear of their own imagined painful death from falling, poisoning, fire, or other external causes.

Adolescence (Philosophical Thinking)

Adolescents grow closer to adult views and experiences of death and can adopt a very philosophical attitude about death. They may idealize the deceased, which can be a problem if the deceased is a peer who has committed suicide. If one parent has died, sometimes adolescents will challenge the surviving parent with statements such as, "Dad would let me do that," when Dad has died and is not available for comment.

The task of adolescence is to separate from one's parents and find support and identity among one's peers. When grief strikes, however, teenagers might want to stay home Friday night instead of going out with friends to enjoy their usual activities. They may feel a need to be close to family, either because they need the support themselves or because they want to support others. Unless they have peers who have suffered a similar loss, most will feel their friends do not understand what they are going through. The greatest fears at this age tend to be of separation and nonexistence.

These guidelines on the developmental stages of understanding death are specific for a school environment: They do not examine developmental changes in perceptions of death after adolescence. But of course our opinions about death and our coping skills with grief continue to change into adulthood as we experience our own aging process and the deaths of others.

Trauma

Trauma is very different from grief. Trauma is a biochemical response in the limbic brain, which mobilizes in response to threat to life or limb. It is a primal reaction to exposure to events beyond the realm of everyday experience, and it has emotional, physical, and behavior components. Often trauma leaves us using maladaptive coping strategies. If a number of people have the same proximity or exposure to a harrowing incident, they will experience very different levels of trauma. For those who do become traumatized, a variety of fears, anxieties, and phobias arise if they do not receive treatment that is specifically effective with psychological trauma. Without treatment, trauma generally does not get better over time.

At least some members of the Safe Room's staff must be skilled in providing interventions for those who are struggling with traumatic reactions. Traditional counseling techniques aimed at supporting emotional well-being are effective for grief victims, but often counterproductive for trauma victims. In the early stages of traumatic reactions, connecting with emotion often brings about a re-experiencing of the trauma. When we try to reach a traumatized person on the emotional level, we often further isolate that person. Staying in a more cognitive mode is usually much more effective.

Memory is stored in the limbic system, without reference to time or place. Because of this, trauma victims are vulnerable to flashbacks even when they are far removed from the traumatic event. A major goal of working with trauma victims is to help them move the memory from the limbic system into the cerebral cortex. Then they have greater control over their thoughts and greater capacity to avoid flashbacks and other uncomfortable traumatic symptoms. Only then can they fully move into the emotional response of grieving.

Often a surprising number of students who are in the Safe Room are actually struggling with the aftermath of trauma, not grief. Any students who were with the student immediately before the death or who witnessed the death will have stronger reactions and have greater needs than others. Proximity to the death is the single greatest indicator of the potential for trauma. Being around grieving students triggers reactions in traumatized students. Some suffer flashbacks and hypervigilance and act out to regain a sense of control. Others withdraw and self-isolate. When the Safe Room staff are trained to recognize the signs of trauma, they can separate traumatized from grieving students—for the benefit of all.

The reactions of others in a crisis can also create the potential for trauma. As mentioned earlier, in any group of people, responses to the same event vary greatly. Times of crisis can bring about increased bonding, cooperation, and support, and deepening relationship, or they may lead to blame, increased conflict, or other destructive reactions. Likewise, an individual's response can also vary: In particular, a child's response to a traumatic event is quite dependent upon the responses of adults around him or her.

Trauma often leaves people feeling helpless and out of control. Consequently, when an adult maintains a sense of control and coaches a child about how to remain safe, the child's response may be, "Sometimes scary things happen, but adults help keep me safe." When the same child suffers the same event under the care of an adult who immediately panics, however, the child interprets the event as one that merits panic. He or she may be left feeling isolated and anxious that in times of greatest need, he or she will be abandoned. In some cases, the child fears for his or her life. The negative reactions people have to trauma and the impact of their reactions on others they love can increase the shattering effects of trauma.

The Developmental Stages of Trauma Response

Trauma rocks us to the core: We fear for our own survival and suddenly question entirely our sense of safety and trust in the world. Traumatic reactions, like responses to grief, vary according to the age and development of the victim.

Under 3 (Preverbal)

At this stage, children may engage in repetitive play, acting out the event and its outcome or fantasized alternative outcomes. They display an anxious attachment to caregivers and may regress emotionally and behaviorally, requiring help with self-care tasks previously mastered, such as brushing teeth, washing, or dressing. Night terrors are not uncommon (and may occur in older children as well).

Ages 3–6 (Preschool–First Grade)

At this stage children begin to verbalize their fears. They often want to avoid objects associated with the trauma. They may regress to earlier behaviors, such as bedwetting, and often become more wary and less prone to smile at strangers. Clinging or wanting to be in close proximity to caregivers is common.

Ages 6–10 (Elementary School)

Grade-school children can be preoccupied with intrusive thoughts and memories about the event; they may talk incessantly about the event or its details. Fantasies about the event with "savior" endings may dominate their talk and play. They can exhibit a loss of short-term memory and have difficulty controlling their behavior (which can interfere with school activities). Preverbal through elementary school–aged children may become withdrawn and quiet, playing and laughing less, even choosing not to speak in an effort to regain control over one part of their lives.

Ages 10–13 (Middle School)

At this stage, children may regress to childlike behaviors and attitudes after a traumatic event. They may express anger about the unfairness of the event and display strong "black and white" judgment about how the disaster was handled and who is to blame. Some are euphoric about having survived the event. Others express interest in omens or "deals": "If I see this sign next time, I'll know what's coming and be able to prevent it," the child reasons, or, "If I make this promise now, I'll have better luck next time." These show that the child recognizes how overwhelming and universal traumatic events are, but has not yet formed mature coping skills. Instead, he or she looks for ways to create a sense of control and distance from the event.

Adolescence (High School)

High school students may show signs of trauma through intensified death-defying or death-denying behavior like driving fast, using drugs, or otherwise "tempting" death. They may exhibit depression or a rebellious attitude (sometimes through acting promiscuously) as a cover for fear. Some students may regress and exhibit nearly any of the behaviors listed above for younger age groups.

Youth of All Ages

Many traumatized children exhibit intensified or exaggerated reactions to certain stimuli (touch, scent, noise, and so on). They may reveal feelings of helplessness or suddenly recognize their dependence upon adults for care and protection. They show low tolerance for changes in routine and cling to predictability and stability. They may experience disturbances in their eating and sleeping habits, suffer psychosomatic illnesses, and show declining grades or difficulty concentrating. They often struggle with flashbacks, nightmares, and disabling anxiety and hyperarousal.

Challenges for the Safe Room

Because of the biochemical changes within the brain for those who have been exposed to traumatic events, adults in the Safe Room will likely be challenged by several behavioral outcomes in children and youth:

- The anxiety students experience often makes them intolerant, on edge, impulsive, irritated, and impatient.

- Their fears and emotions lead them to act out. In a situation that feels out of control, students want adults to set boundaries—they want someone to take control.

- Being around grieving students may trigger flashbacks and other disconcerting cognitive and emotional reactions that make traumatized students even more likely to act out.

- Students cannot express why the Safe Room is not working for them when they are struggling with trauma. Because the experience of trauma is likely new for them and because they lose the ability to use some parts of their brains, they just do not have the capacity to recognize it or to label it.

It is important for Safe Room staff members to realize that for students struggling with trauma, these are not disciplinary problems, but indications of students needing extra attention and, perhaps, referral for professional help. Teachers also need to understand this, because it is counterproductive to discipline these troubled students. Discipline will not change the biochemistry of trauma in their brains or bodies! They need trauma intervention to reconcile the event in a way that does not trigger intense emotions and feelings of helplessness.

Clearly, crisis can produce an incredible range of reactions. A student's age and understanding of death, his or her proximity to the events and persons involved in the crisis, and the environment and reactions of others during and after the crisis can have tremendous impact on that student's response and recovery. An ad-hoc approach to crisis response or to running the Safe Room will simply not be sufficient to meet the needs of students. Adequately teaching the skills for responding to trauma is beyond the scope of a book focused on Safe Rooms, but it is essential that Flight Team members and school counselors know how to differentiate traumatized students from grieving students.

Below is an overview of the differences between grief and trauma. Additionally, some members of the Flight Team must be highly trained in a trauma intervention model designed specifically for use in schools and with students.

Grief	Trauma
• Grief resides in the heart; it is an emotional response.	• Trauma is a brain-based, biochemical, and primal reaction. It is cognitive in nature.
• Only some people experiencing grief will need professional help.	• Survivors of trauma need intervention. Trauma can be seriously disabling if left untreated.
• Grieving usually begins as soon as the initial denial is overcome.	• The trauma victim does not need to know the injured or deceased to suffer trauma.
• Grief is related to a feeling of loss of someone loved or deeply cared about.	• Trauma victims often exhibit new fears, anxieties, or phobias.
• Grieving people often long for an emotional connection.	• Proximity to emotional or grieving people triggers high anxiety in trauma victims.
• Grief needs a witness, a companion, or a compassionate listener.	• Traditional counseling and emotional approaches are usually counterproductive for trauma victims.

Referring Students for Professional Help

There are generally three ways to support traumatized children. First, teachers, parents, and others in their daily lives can provide love and support (they will need guidance on the specific details of trauma's effects). Second, a trained Safe Room team member can provide a child- or survivor-oriented trauma intervention that is appropriate in a school setting. Finally, Safe Room staff can escort students to the school counselor for referral to outside professionals who will provide ongoing therapy.

Safe Room staff members are not expected to have all the answers. Their purpose is ask to students guiding questions, thus permitting youth to develop, discover, and understand their own individual needs. Staff members serve as guideposts at various forks in the road, carefully witnessing student journeys through grief.

Staff must be able to recognize, however, when students are having reactions greater than the situation calls for or real difficulty with the grieving process. These students may not be able to complete the journey without professional help. Safe Room staff must be certain to escort youth at risk of abuse, suicide, mental illness, or other issues to the school counselor. It is not the duty of Safe Room staff to treat these issues—indeed, severe problems are better left to trained specialists who will have a long-term professional relationship with the child—but it is crucial that they identify and refer these students for appropriate care. Safe Room staff and Flight Team members throughout the school must know how to voice their concerns, and they must be able to carefully convey these concerns to school counselors and parents.

If the Safe Room staff has concerns about a child, talk with the school counselor to find out whether he or she is seeing the same signs and whether the parents should be notified. Most parents will welcome honest observations and concern. It is helpful to have a list of resources for parents ready in case they agree with the staff's assessment and want to seek professional help for their child.

Be certain that the professionals your school recommends for ongoing treatment have experience or certification specifically for trauma. Ask potential therapists if they are associated with the International Society for Traumatic Stress Studies (ISTSS), the Academy of Traumatology, or the Green Cross Assistance Program. Ask if they are familiar with trauma techniques such as Eye Movement Desensitization and Reprocessing (EMDR).

Alternatively, give the counselor a hypothetical example of a child who keeps talking about the details of traumatic event over and over, and ask what approach he or she would use. A counselor trained in trauma response would focus on working with the child cognitively to put the event into a broader context. An untrained counselor, by contrast, might suggest that the child needs to keep talking about those events to work through his or her emotions.

For more ways to support students, please refer to the *Crisis Resource Manual.* The next chapter will address training issues for Safe Room staff, and the chapter following that will explore how to implement training to help students process grief.

Signs That a Student May Need Professional Help

Any of the signs listed here can be expected at the onset of grief or trauma. Pay particular attention if these persist over time. Certain symptoms require immediate attention: If children are at risk of hurting themselves or others, do not wait to take action. All staff in Safe Rooms must comply with the mandatory reporting laws for their state and must involve the student's district counselor or administrator. Follow the protocol outlined by your district's policy.

Emotional Signs

- Persistent anxiety
- Hopes for reunion with deceased
- Desire to die
- Clinging to others
- Absence of all grief
- Strong resistance to forming new attachments
- Only negative or only positive expression
- Panic, fear, or terror

Behavioral Signs

- Aggression, displays of power
- Withdrawal, regression
- Overachieving syndrome
- Inability to focus
- Loss of concentration
- Self-destructiveness, self-injury, or self-mutilation
- Low impulse control
- Excessive daydreaming
- Compulsive care-giving
- Suddenly becomes accident-prone
- Stealing and other illegal activities
- Use or abuse of drugs, alcohol, or both
- Inability to speak about the deceased

Physical Signs

- Changes in eating (less or more)
- Changes in sleeping (less or more)
- Significant loss of energy

- Nausea
- Headaches
- Stomachaches
- Changes in hygiene

Cognitive Signs

- Inability to concentrate
- Confused or distorted thinking
- Warped sense of time
- Difficulty with decision-making
- Difficulty with short-term memory

- Repetitive thoughts of the traumatic event
- Persistent thoughts of dread or impending doom
- Flashbacks, nightmares, or lack of control over thoughts

Chapter 4

Safe Room Training

• • • • • • • • • • • • • • • • • •

TRAINING

Because a variety of specific psychological needs arise in the Safe Room, as the previous chapter demonstrated, those operating the Safe Room must be highly skilled and trained. There is no substitute for professional training in crisis management and trauma response. The exercises in this chapter are in no way intended to replace professional training; that is beyond the scope of this book. Instead, the activities presented in this chapter will help individuals and teams gain insights about their own grief processes and will give them concepts and language that are helpful in the Safe Room.

The Power of Training

Often Safe Room team members publicly acknowledge that training is "a good idea," but privately feel that they personally do not need training because their expertise includes understanding ways to help those who grieve. This is especially true if the school staffs the Safe Room with mental health practitioners from local agencies in addition to counselors from neighboring schools or districts.

But training for Safe Room staff does not center on grief. Grief will be covered, for sure, but a far more important point of training is to make absolutely certain that everyone supports a shared philosophy, knows the protocol, understands the process, and respects the chain of command, particularly the site administrator or principal's ultimate authority over his or her school. The Safe Room is not a place for "wild cards" on the staff. Without policy, procedures, guidelines, or protocols in place, it will be very difficult to keep control over the Safe Room. If the Flight Team is not invited back the next time a crisis occurs, students will suffer the consequences.

The training for Safe Rooms does not require an unreasonable commitment of time; at the Crisis Management Institute, Safe Room training is 1 day of a 5-day Flight Team (crisis response team) training. After a 5-day training, refreshers and update trainings need to occur annually, with additional opportunities for team members to gather and process what has been learned from each response and to revise and improve their plans.

Keys to a Successful Safe Room

1. **Efficient handling of information.** The Safe Room functions best when school staff briefs the Flight Team members on the building layout, history, and other important specifics. Local school staff will also have insights into groups of students who might need special attention, such as those who were active in extracurricular activities with the deceased or missing student.

2. **A high level of training, practice, and skill.** The Rapid Response and Flight Team members must receive professional training. Regular refresher training is essential to maintain high team skills. This is another reason to encourage administrators to mobilize the team even when the deceased child was not well-known: Practicing on a single tragedy allows us to refine our plans before a catastrophe that requires our best response.

3. **Effective behavior management.** Safe Room staff must be able to manage student behavior in the Safe Room. Capable handling of student behavior establishes an environment that permits students to feel safe and to grieve.

4. **Educated needs assessment.** To successfully meet student needs, Safe Room staff must clearly understand the developmental stages of the children in the room. They must clearly understand the difference between grief and trauma and be prepared to offer trauma intervention, and they must recognize children in need of professional help and follow through with referrals.

TRAINING

A Whole-School Approach

Crisis response and trauma intervention skills are tremendously valuable beyond meeting the immediate needs of students in crisis for information, emotional support, and empathy.

Students may experience private loss at any time during the year: the death of a parent, sibling, or other significant family member; divorce; or even the death of a much-beloved pet. School staff can have a profound, positive impact on student recovery from these private tragedies.

For this reason, Safe Room training must be a part of the overall crisis response organization of the school, and ongoing training has to be a strong point of advocacy for all school staff—not just among team members. Crisis response training should not be limited to the crisis response team, nor should Safe Room training be limited to future Safe Room coordinators: All Flight Team members should receive Safe Room training, and all school staff should be subsequently inserviced in portions of the crisis response training that enhance their skills and understanding. The Flight Team will not be called out to help a single child who has suffered a loss unrelated to school (such as the death of a parent), but individual staff members may need to respond to a student who is experiencing distress. Their response can make a powerful difference in that child's adjustment and recovery. Teachers, counselors, and coaches all touch children's lives.

The Role of Teachers

Teachers in particular are key players in students' lives and can play a crucial role in student coping and recovery following crises and tragedies. Because teachers handle the classroom announcement of a crisis to students, their portrayal of the Safe Room sets the tone for whether students will be respectful of others, will feel free to use the Safe Room, or will tease those who do. Therefore, it is crucial that teachers are "on board" with the concepts of the Safe Room and are willing to be supportive in their representation. Provide crisis training to teachers to help them understand that the Safe Room will:

- Allow classrooms to return to normalcy more quickly.

- Provide an opportunity for students to come to terms with major life issues and challenges.

- Teach students coping skills that help in the current situation and will form the foundation for coping with grief for the rest of their lives.

- Enhance crisis response efforts.

- Send students the message—when the Safe Room is opened after a less popular or little-known child dies— that the lives of all students matter.

- Send the message that school staff care about kids and about their well-being.

- Aid in detecting and helping students who may be on the edge or need professional help.

Be sure that teachers know, too, that the Safe Room will not be a place to go if students want to cut class: Students will be sent back to class as soon as they have done their current grief work.

A Personal Challenge

Safe Room skills are also important for events that challenge us personally, outside the school setting, at all age levels. In fact, the best preparation Safe Room staff can do and the greatest gift

TRAINING

they can give those they will serve in the Safe Room is to do their own grief work *before* crisis strikes. The strength we gain by reconciling our own losses is a great ally in our mission to support others. Those who have not adequately addressed their own grief may find themselves unable to truly be there for others who are grieving. There are many ways of working through these personal issues. Churches and counseling offices offer grief support groups for those who have suffered a specific loss.

Others may be uncomfortable in the Safe Room due to lack of experience with death and loss. Our culture helps us avoid grief: We tend to hire other people for many of the tasks and responsibilities for caring for the dying and deceased. But we can learn a great deal from relationships with the dying. Consider volunteering to work with hospice patients. When the dying person is not a family member, the loss is still painful, but we can gain enough distance to think about it from a more philosophical place, which prepares us better for when the loss is very personal.

In addition, hospices and other organizations often offer support groups for grieving children, and they look for adults they can train to lead those groups. Both the training and the experience of facilitating those groups would be very helpful in understanding how the Safe Room operates and what the needs of children are in the aftermath of a death of a friend. With practice, serving others as a companion in grief becomes more comfortable.

Activities for Safe Room Staff and Crisis Team Members

This section offers a few activities that can be used with Safe Room staff for continuing education or used independently for personal growth. Most of these activities can also be used with students in the Safe Room and with students in the classroom with the empty desk (where the deceased or missing classmate used to sit). These activities may help the class and the teacher work together on their grief.

When we train crisis response teams at a Crisis Management Institute workshop, we devote less than a third of the time to lectures or direct instruction. The remaining time is committed to small group exercises, large group discussion, scenario work, and other integrated, dynamic learning. The goal is to turn the concepts discussed into skills. Safe Room coordinators and other team leaders can learn a great deal from doing these activities individually, before offering them to other groups. Almost all of us experience "Aha!" moments—discoveries about ourselves—while exploring the activities and questions presented here. With newly revealed insights, the Safe Room coordinator and other Flight Team members are better prepared to determine which activities might be most effective in the Safe Room, and under what circumstances.

When leading a group through these activities, begin the session by speaking about the importance of confidentiality. Ask people to indicate their willingness to keep all things said by those in the group confidential. Point out that supporting each other on deeper levels in the safety of a training session makes everyone better able to assist students and staff in the midst of a crisis. If we are unable to support each other here and now, one might suggest, how can we expect to be effective with students when they are grieving?

Be sure to end group activities with some large-group discussion of any "Aha!" moments or realizations that group members may be willing to share. Deep work needs words, and group members will need an opportunity to share with others how the exercises have affected them and what they have learned. The activity times are estimates; the actual time may be much longer, depending on the size of the group and participants' willingness to share.

Activity 1: Assessing Staff Readiness (25 minutes)
(For Staff—Group Work)

Allow ample time for participants to write out the answers to the following questions, then break large groups into smaller groups to allow participants to delve into their thoughts out loud and share responses with each other. Give each person equal time to talk in the small groups. End with a whole-group discussion.

Anticipating Personal Reactions

Ask participants who have never worked in a Safe Room to consider the following questions:

1. How comfortable are you being part of a Safe Room team that helps youth process their grief?

2. What could students say that would be difficult for you to hear? Why?

3. What words or actions could you use to best alleviate their pain?

4. How could you show support without using words?

5. What experiences did you have when you were young that you could draw upon when assisting students in the Safe Room?

6. Describe the reactions—both positive and negative— of the adults around you when you endured those experiences.

7. How comfortable are you in maintaining your silence when something deep and painful has just been said? How can you gain the skill of simply listening—of "holding a compassionate space" where the speaker can pause to absorb and comprehend his or her emotions and experience—without commenting or otherwise using words to lessen your own discomfort?

Reviewing Past Experience

Ask participants who have worked in a Safe Room a few times to consider the following questions:

1. What were the most crucial steps in setting up the Safe Room?

2. What are the most important things to do?

3. How would you help a reluctant administrator see the value of having a Safe Room?

4. What are your greatest concerns about Safe Rooms?

5. How do you offer a break from the stress of crisis response to teachers and other staff?

Ask participants to list and prioritize the things that make a Safe Room more efficient and effective.

Pinpointing Critical Skills and Techniques

Ask participants who have worked in Safe Rooms many times to consider the following questions:

1. What would you do if behaviors began to escalate in the Safe Room?

2. What might you try if the staff-to-student ratio is inadequate and student behavior becomes difficult to manage?

3. Under what conditions would you decide to close a Safe Room?

4. What could you tell teachers to help curb their tendency to be gatekeepers or to screen which students "really" need to go to the Safe Room?

5. Are there any unique ideas from your previous experience in Safe Rooms that could help in future Safe Rooms?

Activity 2: The Lovre Bucket Theory (25 minutes)
(For Staff or Students—Group Work)

Pass out blank pieces of paper and writing utensils. Ask participants to think of several losses—the losses do not have to be deaths—that they have sustained during their lives.

Ask participants to imagine that there is a make-believe bucket of tears inside each of us that represents the grief we feel when we experience a personal loss. At first, the bucket is very full, and tears readily spill out over the top. As time passes, however, we process our grief and the level of tears decreases, creating "jiggle space" at the top of the bucket—unless we repress or deny our emotions. When there is only a little jiggle space, nearly every upset in life has the potential to make us "spill" tears, because we have less resilience than usual. Then a rather common daily challenge can "bump" the bucket, causing tears to spill out, sometimes unexpectedly. The more tears we let out, the more jiggle space we create—and the more easily we can handle daily disappointments.

Instruct participants to draw a bucket for each loss they have experienced, to write a name for the person or incident on each bucket, and to draw the level of tears they have left inside the bucket regarding that loss. Then ask participants to write in the remaining space about what helped at the time of the loss, what else would have helped, and what could be done now to lower the level of tears.

For those more stoic individuals who do not cry or relate by means of tears, the activity leader might ask, "What is your bucket filled with instead?" It could be filled with anger or another displaced emotion, but the same analogy may well apply: When something or somebody "bumps" their bucket and some of it spills out, what happens next? Students, for example, may realize that they pick fights to dissipate anger or victimize other children to feel powerful or in control. Adults might see other ways that their repressed grief spills over and causes reactions elsewhere.

Take some time to examine with everyone how it is different to empty a bucket filled with anger. With sadness and tears, letting it out and giving it voice provides relief, but with anger, letting it out might mean throwing bean bags against a wall or using a punching bag. The practice of acting out angrily can simply become a habit, however, and a means for hiding from the emotions far beneath the anger. It is important to help participants find support if they are working on these kinds of issues.

After the drawing and general discussion, pose the following questions:

1. What insights about yourself did you gain from doing this exercise?

2. What else did you discover as you gave thought to this exercise?

3. What did you learn from listening to others discuss this exercise?

4. What did you discover that was most surprising to you?

Then pass out new pieces of paper and ask participants to consider how they might use the bucket concept to represent multiple losses associated with a particular death or major change. For example, imagine the child whose father has died: The family loses their home and must move to an apartment, the child loses contact with friends and must attend a new school, and so forth. The activity leader can give an example from his or her own life or draw an example from someone else who is struggling with a major challenge or life change. Ask participants to represent the "fallout" or ripple effect associated with one major loss.

Ask some of the participants to share any major "Aha!" moments or revelations they had with the whole group; then allow participants to debrief in pairs or small groups.

Activity 3: Map of Grief (25 minutes) (For Staff or Students—Group Work)

This activity acknowledges that the process of reconciling loss and grief is like a journey. It graphically displays that we each have our own unique process; no person's journey will look precisely like another's.

Give each participant a blank sheet of paper and these simple instructions: "Draw a map of your journey through grief." Provide a variety of colored pencils or felt pens. Each color can represent something specific about the journey. If an array of colored writing instruments is not available, simple pen and paper will work.

If participants ask questions about this exercise, simply indicate that it is fine to do anything they like to represent the process—from drawing symbols that have special meaning only to them to simply listing the many steps taken on their journey, including the amount of time spent at certain stages. Lines on their maps might resemble flow charts or forest pathways; they might use forks at places of challenge. There are no limits to how the participants can put their journeys on paper.

Give the participants the opportunity to reflect and draw or write. After about 10 minutes, tell them they have "2 more minutes to finish." Then let them break into pairs or small groups and share with each other what they illustrated and what they have learned. Be sure to allow enough time to give everyone a chance to share; consider putting participants in pairs or very small groups if time is limited. Encourage participants not to interrupt or ask questions as long as the one sharing keeps talking. This is a time to teach the listening partner to truly focus and listen. Allow at least 3 to 5 minutes per person, depending on age: In a student group, older students will have more ability for verbal expression and will benefit from more time.

For those who are not accustomed to this kind of sharing, the activity leader might initiate this task by sharing some ideas concerning his or her own map:

- "What surprised me in doing this was _____."
- "Something I learned in this process is _____."
- *[For staff]* "This would be valuable to use in the Safe Room when _____."

Even when people begin to talk about how they would use this activity with others, it is likely that many individuals will also relate their personal experiences in their small groups. If someone has an urgent personal issue, that private work should take priority over the goals of the activity. After all, if we cannot support each other during training, how will we able to support each other and our students in an actual Safe Room?

End the session with large group discussion in which you ask participants to complete the statements mentioned earlier. In Crisis Management Institute training sessions, we often ask participants if they would be willing to share their maps so that all can see the variety of ways this process can be illustrated.

Activity 4: Circles of Support (25 minutes)
(For Staff or Students—Group or Individual Work)

Distribute copies of the reproducible Circles of Support handout (page 83) to participants and instruct them to label the top set of circles "At work" (staff) or "At school" (students). The lower set of circles should be labeled "In my personal life" for both groups. For each setting, ask participants to write the names of two or three people who are their 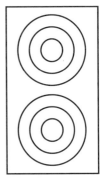 very closest advisors or confidants in the center circle. In the middle ring, participants should write the names of people who are helpful, but not their first choice in tough times. The outer ring should contain the names of those who give sound advice, but are just a little further out in terms of choice. Allow 5–7 minutes for this portion of the activity.

When it looks like people are finished, break the session into smaller groups. Allow participants 20 minutes or so to debrief their own support systems and experience.

Encourage staff members to discuss the importance of everyone understanding these concepts—their closest confidants, their next-closest confidants, and so forth—not only in their personal lives, but especially when working with students in Safe Rooms.

For students, use this exercise as a discussion starter: It can show us whether students have a support network and whether they recognize it as such. This exercise also reinforces trust.

Safe Room coordinators and members of the Rapid Response and Flight Teams need to be familiar with a variety of activities like these and to have a clear sense of each activity's function in the grief process. This allows Safe Room staff to choose activities in the Safe Room that are suited to the needs of individual children rather than assuming one activity will be helpful for all. Having such activities available helps the Safe Room staff to "hit the ground running" when managing behaviors and assisting students as they work through their grief. Chapter 6 (page 111) contains many activities that students and staff will find helpful. The next chapter explores how staff can use conversations with students in the Safe Room to determine their needs and the most appropriate activities.

Circles of Support

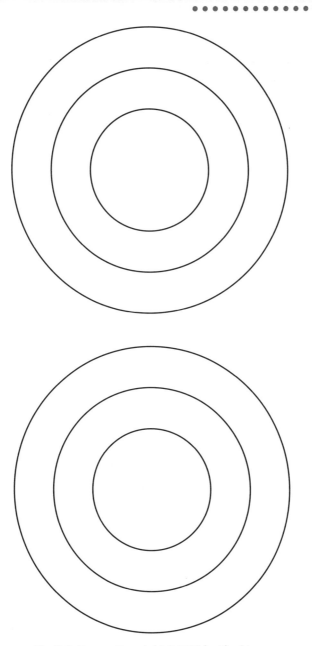

Chapter 5

Helping Students Process Grief

PROCESSNG GRIEF

The Safe Room is a special space where students can process grief of all kinds. Grief does not need answers, advice, or someone to tell the griever how to feel; grief needs a witness. The greatest gift we can give people in this kind of pain is to be fully present but silent, to simply bear witness to the process and support them as they walk into the deepest well of their lives.

Adults are often uncomfortable with this kind of silence. When students say things that are emotionally raw or filled with terror and rage, we tend to fill up the space with words of advice, affirmation, reflection—any words will do—in the hope that words will heal or at least cloak our own dread and fears. We squirm, wiggle, and struggle with the desire to say something that will take away the pain.

But in reality, nothing we say can help others get around or avoid pain. People in grief benefit by moving through their pain one step at a time; they are strengthened by their capacity to do it themselves—with support from those they trust—and they learn something in the process about how they might bear witness for another person's grief at a future time. Deep into the heart of pain is exactly where the grieving person needs to go.

The Safe Room is an opportunity for adults to witness and affirm a young person making this difficult journey for what may be the first time and discovering his or her own integrity and dignity.

Assess Student Needs

As previous chapters have made clear, students come to the Safe Room with a variety of needs, and it is vital that staff are able to assess and meet those needs. The first step in the assessment process is for the greeter who meets students at the door to ask a few questions and help them choose where to sit once they have signed in.

The answers to a few questions can reveal whether a student would be better served by joining a group of other students (and if so, which group) or by individual counseling. For instance, simply asking, "Did you know Jimmy *[the boy who died]*, or did you come down for some other reason?" or saying, "There are many reasons why students have come in today. Can you help me understand what is happening for you?" will give staff an immediate sense of where each child is in the grief process.

Five Categories of Students in the Safe Room

Students who use the Safe Room generally fall into five groups:

1. Students who are in shock. The most obvious group appears to be in shock when they arrive at the Safe Room. These are usually the students who have just learned that someone they love or care about has died. They need time to react and to be "pretty blown away" before they are ready to begin processing the loss. Anything Safe Room staff can do to help those students find words for what they are experiencing will help them move beyond the initial denial. They need time with other friends of the deceased to share memories, to express their sadness, and to make memorial plans. Do not push too soon, and help these students find their natural groupings.

2. Students who have suffered an unrelated loss. A second group arrives crying or looking as if they have been crying for weeks. They tend to be students suffering an unrelated loss, such as the death of a parent or sibling. The unrelated death may have occurred quite some time ago, but the current tragedy has triggered memories and brought them to the surface. They may benefit by being grouped with students who have experienced a similar loss. Often these students have been in school for weeks, months, or even years since their personal loss, and their grief may not have been evident until this new loss. But seeing others grieve can touch that place within themselves. A fair number of students with unrelated losses visit the Safe Room.

3. Students who have problems at home. There is also often a number of students who have a critical personal issue other than a death-related loss, such as sexual abuse or domestic violence in their homes. The Safe Room affords a secure place for those students who have never disclosed their family history, the dynamics of their situation, or (in some cases) their suicidal thoughts.

These students do not need to talk to other students; they need one-to-one adult attention and support and referral to the school counselor. Let students be in charge of their feelings. Ask each student if he or she would like to meet privately with a counselor. Walk him or her to the counselor's office, and wait there with the student until the counselor is available.

Student: "I've never told anyone this stuff about my dad."

Safe Room staff member: "You know, what you are saying is so important. I won't be here tomorrow, but I know this won't be over for you by then. Would you like to walk down to the counselor's office and let her know what's going on?"

These students may also need appropriate referrals to professionals and outside agencies. The Safe Room team should keep a list of students who express disconcerting thoughts or emotions or who seem particularly withdrawn. They may need follow-up or a referral (see "Signs That a Student May Need Professional Help," page 65).

4. Students who tend to spin out of control any time the school environment is destabilized. There are students, often from dysfunctional families, who will "spin out" at every chaotic event. They, too, may have some major life issue that they can deal with if allowed a short time in the Safe Room. The destabilized environment of a crisis—which may be similar to the chaos they feel at home, rather than the stability they are used to at school—can bring their difficulties to the surface. These students may be able to work in small groups, but will probably need fairly close supervision, guidance, and interaction with Safe Room staff. If given the chance, they can regain control and improve their reactions to crisis situations. This is an opportunity to teach them new coping skills.

5. Students who are curious. Some students will simply be curious about what is going on in the Safe Room. As long as their behavior is appropriate, permit them to choose how long they stay. They can get a terrific lesson in compassion. Over time, these good learning experiences will accumulate and affect school climate in a positive way. Students begin to understand the universality of death and grief and learn to support one another. These experiences are the seeds from which empathy grows.

PROCESSNG GRIEF

Diffuse the Drama

Some students come to the Safe Room to support their friends, which is great. Others show up for the drama, and that is not. To deal with this challenge:

- Separate "drama-seeking students" from others so they get less attention from their peers.

- Break these students into smaller groups. Divide and conquer!

- Be candid and direct.

- Make statements of observation: "Sometimes students become overly dramatic at times like this simply to get attention or to be sure others know that they are troubled by the loss." Additionally, you might say, "Some of your reactions appear to me to be rather dramatic. Help me understand what is happening for you."

Opening Gambits

After students sign in and review the rules, some students will find natural groupings and begin to talk with peers. Sometimes the most difficult part of working in the Safe Room, however, is helping students begin to talk. Some are in that quiet place of shock—not clinical shock, but emotional shock—and are unable to begin the process of grieving, especially if they did not know about the death until the teacher read the announcement. It is fine to give students a little time to sit silently, but at some point, a staff member should attempt to engage the child.

For those students who are not talking with peers, here are some suggested "openers" for Safe Room staff:

- "I am glad you came in. I'm sorry this has happened to you [*or to your school*]."

- "How did you know _____? How did you learn of _____'s death?"

- "Yes, what happened is horrible. Things may never seem the same, but they can be okay again—given time and support, and your ability to deal with your grief."

- "Did you know _____, or are you feeling sad about someone else's death?"

- "I didn't know _____. Can you tell me what [*he or she*] was like?"

- "What are some of your favorite memories of _____? What will you miss most?"

- "What is the most painful part about this right now?"

Avoid meaningless platitudes or phrases such as:

- "I know how you feel."

- "He led a good, long life."

- "It was God's will."

- "At least she didn't suffer."

Always remember that though it is not always comfortable to do, sometimes it is most effective and helpful to simply sit silently for a time with those who need your help.

Building Empathy

This scenario shows how Safe Room staff can use a student's curiosity to create a learning experience.

A student whips in the door and eyes the treats across the room.

Safe Room staff member: "Looks like you found the treats!"

Student: "Yep, I heard there were snacks in here."

Safe Room staff member: "So, go ahead and get one and bring it over here."

[A few moments later]

Safe Room staff member: "Did you know Joey, the boy who died? No? Well, have you ever had someone in your family die?"

Student: "Actually, I've never known anyone who's died."

Safe Room staff member: "See the students at that table over there? They all lost a grandparent. What kinds of feelings do you think kids have when a grandparent dies? And that table? Those kids all knew Joey. Can you imagine how sad it would be to lose a friend?"

The staff member uses guiding questions to find ways to connect the student to what is happening in the Safe Room. Since the child does not have any unresolved loss that can be identified, the staff member then tries to help him or her feel empathy for others who are grieving.

Follow the LOVRE Model

One easy way of remembering what to do in the Safe Room—how to respond, what to say, what not to say—is to remember the letter sequence L-O-V-R-E: *Listen, Observe, Validate, Reflect,* and *Empathize.*

Listen

When people are asked who gave them the most support during a really difficult time in their lives, nearly all say that it was someone who was a good listener. Seldom does one hear it was "the person who gave me answers" or "the person who gave the best advice." One of the tasks of grief is to put words to our loss. Doing so with someone who *listens* with compassion allows us to sort through what the loss means *to us.* It helps us to see how we will begin to cope and adjust. Be the learner, rather than the teacher: Observe a student's process, rather than counseling or advising. Listen more than you speak!

In the Safe Room, just listen if a student is talking. Nod. Keep comfortable eye contact by not staring, but not entirely averting eye contact, either. Say "Mm hmm," and nod again. Unless the student is saying things that raise concern for bodily harm, just listen. Do not rush to rearrange the student's thought process. Let his or her thoughts wander, and allow the student to fully investigate the meaning of the loss.

Observe

Even being asked a question does not require an answer. Rather, it may warrant validation or perhaps more exploration. Sometimes the most effective response to a student's question is to pause, nod, and ask or state something that encourages the child to go deeper or to clarify his or her query:

- "I've wondered about that as well. When have you had these kinds of thoughts before?"

- "Sometimes questions that come up at times like this are the biggest, deepest kinds of questions we can have. How else might we go about looking at this?"

- "Do you have a mentor? Do you know what a mentor is? What would someone wise say to you right now?"

- "What do you think other students might be thinking about that?"

Statements of observation are helpful if a student "shuts down" or is too withdrawn to begin speaking. This approach draws out conversation without being confrontational:

- "This is such a difficult time."

- "I don't know when I've been at a school that was so filled with students grieving."

- "Sometimes it is so difficult to find words."

Validate

Validation comes in many forms. Sometimes just nodding will do, but finding words that help students know that their reactions are not surprising can also offer validation.

Sometimes this is called "normalizing" reactions, but it is important to avoid using the word "normal." Often people say, "Yours is a normal reaction to an abnormal event." This comment can be more damaging than helpful. Grieving people often feel *entirely abnormal,* and hearing otherwise leaves them feeling even more misunderstood and alone. Try other ways of communicating that grief is a natural response:

- "I've heard others say the same kind of thing today."

- "Given what you've survived, it doesn't surprise me that you'd be feeling that way."

Reflect

After listening, observing, and validating the student's experience and feelings, the adult can allow the student time to reflect on the deeper meaning of the death and to put words to what he or she has learned from the conversation. This is that moment when an adult might lean back and recall earlier experiences in his or her own life that might be similar to the student's experience—not to start a new conversation, but to create an open space in which the student can share his or her reflections on how the death or tragedy might affect life in the future.

It takes a certain presence for us to support people in the Safe Room; often, being successful at it depends on our ability to connect with something inside that gave us sustenance during our own painful times. The point, however, is for the adult to relate personal experiences that connect to the situation in a way that *does not* express his or her own grief or make the student feel the need to take care of the adult:

- "I remember when a boy died during my high school years. Our school didn't know what to do. But I remember how upset we all were."

- "You know, I remember how powerfully a drunk-driving accident affected me and my friends when we were your age."

Supporters need to recognize that they are witnessing someone else's pain, not their own. As adults, we know from experience that listening to words of fear and anguish often triggers painful recollections and reawakens our own unresolved grief. The discussion of training in chapter 4 noted that one of the most important things Safe Room staff members can do to prepare for student grief is to deal with their personal grief first. Only then will they be able to listen, observe, validate, and reflect to their full capacity.

Empathize

The final step in the process is for us to empathize with students. The experience of receiving empathy teaches students how to give empathy: Students learn that we do not have to share the same experiences and feelings to relate to another person's pain in a supportive way. Empathy allows us to form deep connections. When a student has received appropriate care in the Safe Room, he or she can listen to another student process his or her grief, and together they can find common sources of support and create a space that facilitates the grieving process for both of them. The value of this lesson far outlasts a single tragedy. The ability to empathize will be an important lifelong skill.

Speak the Truth—With Care

As chapter 3 discussed, children need to know the truth about the death. A pivotal element of training for Safe Room team members involves learning techniques for dealing with unknowns like a missing student or difficult truths like homicide, suicide, abuse, and drunk driving. It is always more difficult for students when all of the facts about the crisis or death are unknown, or when the death was caused by human intent (homicide or suicide). Secrets and rumors only generate more anxiety. Clarify the facts as far as possible, and then focus on the students' feelings.

If there are aspects of the death or event that are too gory or for some other reason too difficult to talk about, it is better to be honest about that than to whitewash the event with a cover story. This shows respect for the students' integrity and is essential for the credibility of Safe Room staff. It is better to say, "I am not able to say" or, "We're waiting for the police report to verify details about that" than to give false statements. If we are dishonest, we fail to uphold the child's dignity, and we may never gain back the child's trust.

Speak the truth about the deceased, too. It is not helpful to idealize the person who has died. If students or staff are presenting the deceased as a superhuman angel of some kind, point out that he or she was just human like the rest of us and had strengths and weaknesses. Help students realize that making someone else sound perfect is not what makes us miss them: It is the loss of mutual love and caring that brings the pain of grief.

When dealing with ambiguous or unusual situations in which a student expresses guilt or culpability, help the student explore those reactions and try to learn more about his or her actual role. Never simply say, "It wasn't your fault" to someone who actually believes he or she may have any responsibility, and be careful about introducing aspects of the death that might point to carelessness or suggest blame. Even if there was no intent of harm, when a student feels any sort of connection to the death, it is important that someone with professional training evaluate whether this student needs a referral for additional mental health support.

In most cases, a student's feelings of guilt reflect a wish that he or she could have prevented the death. For instance, a student may feel guilty if a friend dies after the student heard the friend say he or she was thinking about suicide, did not realize it was a serious threat, and did not tell an adult. Through careful questions and listening, however, a Safe Room staff member might be able to help the student recognize that he or she is not responsible for the death.

In other cases, a student may feel culpable for more tangible reasons. If the deceased died in a drunk-driving accident, a student who was in the same car and also drunk has an entirely different relationship to the death than a student who was drunk at the same party, but not in the car. When the nature of the student's role is in doubt, referral to the onsite school counselor is advisable. In the meantime, focus on common reactions to the loss of a friend (sadness and loneliness, for example), rather than on the mode of death (which may be the source of guilt). This is only a short-term technique, however. Students with a real connection to the cause of death should be referred to the school counselor or other professional help for long-term support.

Safe Room staff need to know when and how to guide conversations in a positive direction when they falter or slide too far

Finding the "Right" Words

- Try to avoid judgment words like "good," "bad," "right," "wrong," "should," "ought," and "fault." In fact, avoid these words in *all* situations!

- Remember that the words "good," "bad," "right," and "wrong" convey judgment. There are always more effective words to use. Rather than saying, "That was a bad decision," you might say, "There were consequences to your decision that you didn't anticipate," or you might question whether the decision was "mindful" or "thoughtful." Focus on concepts such as whether the action or decision was creative, responsible, respectful, or helpful. These words are more descriptive and less judgmental.

- Asking why often puts people on the defensive, as though they have to defend their emotions or reactions. "Tell me more about that" and "Help me understand how you came to that decision" are ways of asking for the same information in a softer manner.

- "Should" and "ought" are usually parent-like directives. The wisdom students achieve is far more enduring if clarifying questions help them reach their *own* conclusions.

into negative territory. If the conversation seems to be "going south," you might interject comments or questions that redirect the conversation. Begin by validating what the student is saying during a couple of exchanges to build rapport and trust and show that you really are listening and believe that what he or she tells you is true at that moment:

Student: "A bunch of us were together at a party, and we were all talking about killing ourselves. We didn't mean it; it was just talk. But then she went home and did this. It really was our fault for putting that idea into her head."

Safe Room staff member: "I've often heard other students feel responsible for the decisions that a student makes at times like this."

Student: "Yeah, we were all talking about it—kind of egging each other on and each of us talking about how life sucks."

Safe Room staff member: "I think that it is common for kids to get into a place of confirming to each other that there really are difficult parts to being a teenager today. But talking about it didn't make *you* go home and do that. It's important for us to recognize that our words and actions have consequences, and I really appreciate your awareness of that, but it takes more than one person and one event for someone to decide to do something like this."

Then turn the conversation:

Student: "I think she'd still be here if we hadn't gone there that night."

Safe Room staff member: "That is a common misperception. But what we know from people who really study this stuff is that kids who decide to kill themselves don't do that spontaneously very often. Usually they think about it for a long time. How could you know if someone has been thinking about it for a long time?"

It is important to stress that no single person could say or do anything that would make someone else kill him- or herself. There may be exceptions to this, but those exceptions would be for students who live with extreme abuse or some other entirely overwhelming life circumstance. Generally, suicide is the culmination of a history of using thoughts of suicide to gain a sense of empowerment or control over situations or people. Often, when the Flight Team responds to a school after a suicide, students mention signals that their peer gave—but students are not trained to recognize those signals and do not know how to intervene to save a life, nor should they bear that responsibility. Teach students that the best way to help a suicidal friend is to involve adults.

Watch for Warning Signs

Some students may come to the Safe Room because of unrelated issues such as sexual abuse, child abuse, or other fallout from dysfunctional home lives. These students need one-to-one attention from the school counselor and professional referral.

When you are talking to a student about his or her private life, if you suspect any kind of trouble at home, allow the student to self-disclose by asking broad, open-ended questions. Ask, "What's troubling you?" rather than, "Is something wrong with your home life?" This gives the student a sense of control over the conversation. It also improves the school's position if professional referral or a conversation with parents becomes necessary.

For instance, if a girl discloses that a nasty divorce is upsetting her, the school can tell her parents, "Sometimes, in the aftermath of a tragic event, children reveal other things that are troubling them, and in this case, your child revealed that the divorce proceedings are causing her some distress." Parents need assurance that the disclosure was spontaneous and unprompted by "leading questions" or a "nosy" approach. Of course, in cases when legal action against parents may be required as a result of the disclosure, protecting the child's welfare must take priority. But by allowing students to self-disclose, the school protects itself and its students in a manner that is respectful to all parties.

Other students may come to the Safe Room to self-disclose thoughts of suicide. Listen for language that indicates a student may be contemplating suicide or other destructive thoughts:

Student: "I'm so blown away that I'm beginning to question why I think life is worth living."

Safe Room staff member: "I'm always very concerned when students say things like that. Tell me more."

Student: "Well, she was really bright and popular. She had a lot going for her that I don't have. If she didn't think life was worth living, what am I doing here?"

Safe Room staff member: "It is pretty easy to want to compare ourselves to others. But she might have had all kinds of challenges that we don't know about."

The person in the Safe Room who is handling suicide assessments should immediately be connected with any student who has revealed the kind of reasoning shown in the preceding example. It is not essential that all Safe Room staff are trained to do the suicidal assessment, but all need to recognize warning signs and refer the student to the person in the Safe Room who is trained and ready.

Engage the student in a few exchanges to get a sense of where he or she is coming from, and always take threats and language seriously. Ask:

- "Is this the first time you've had these kinds of thoughts?"

- "What do you think about when you're waiting to fall asleep at night?"

- "How often do you have thoughts like this?"

- "Do you think about how you would do it? Do you have a plan?"

Although professionals use some of these questions to determine whether children are suicidal, Safe Room staff can use them for reasons other than assessment. These questions allow you to build trust with students by showing that you are really listening and taking them seriously. Asking questions reassures students that you will not abandon them out of fear of their suicidal tendencies. Their answers also provide valuable information for the school counselor or administrator who will take over the professional referral process.

If a student is determined to be at risk for suicide, be sure to walk that student to the counselor's office. Wait with the student until the counselor is available; do not send suicidal students to the office alone. All referrals need to be implemented by the Safe Room staff making a formal, written referral to the proper school personnel in strict accordance with school procedure; be sure to train all staff members in local school protocol and on the signs that a student may need professional referral (see page 65).

Watch, too, for kids who seem to feel the need to *do* something. Invite them to help plan the school memory event for the deceased, and offer suggestions that will allow them to express themselves creatively (see chapter 6, page 111).

Walk It Off

Grieving students have a wide range of needs, including the need to deal with excess energy. If possible, provide walking or other forms of physical exertion as a helpful alternative to Safe Room activities that involve talking or writing.

If there is a lot of physical energy in the Safe Room, consider taking a group of students to the gym to shoot baskets for a while. Grief creates anxiety, and physical exercise can provide relief. This is especially true of students who witnessed the death and may be experiencing psychological trauma.

Encourage students to take a recess or lunch break to let off energy and regain some sense of normalcy. Children can sometimes move in and out of grieving rather quickly, with many transitions in a single day. Their laughter is not disrespectful: Play is a healthy, temporary reprieve from pain. All students should be encouraged to enjoy the parts of life that they can. Be there to support them when they move back into their grief. Try to get students to express their feelings through drawing pictures or writing letters. Have a variety of activities available so students will have choices to assist in their processing (see chapter 6, page 111).

An Emotional Marathon

A high school student named Mary Ann died in a car accident when her car hit a patch of ice and spun out of control and into a deep ravine. Jared, her boyfriend of more than a year, came into the Safe Room on the first day after Mary Ann's death and was restless, crying, and pacing. A Flight Team member, a runner known as "Michael, the Marathon Man," responded to Jared's need by suggesting that he slip on his running shoes and go for a walk with Jared. They logged miles and miles together on the school's athletic field that day. As they circled the track, Jared never stopped talking—about Mary Ann and about his loss. The walking was more than just good exercise; it was incredibly therapeutic for Jared.

Provide Extra Support

Some groups of students may require extra support:

- The classroom (or classrooms, in the case of middle and high schools) where the deceased child would have been present

- Teams or extracurricular activity groups (including those outside the school setting) to which the student belonged

- Closest friends, and also enemies, of the deceased

- Students who have had unrelated but similar life experiences

- Students who are at risk of suicide or self-injury

Flight Team members may want to separate these students from other groups and gather them into their own space, such as an empty classroom. There they can take some time to process what this loss means for them personally and as a group. The process is the same as mentioned previously:

Listen: "We wanted to pull you all together since Sean played on the team with you. We knew that this would be a really tough day. What kinds of things come up for you as you think about this?"

Observe: "I can see on your faces that this is such a big loss for you. You all played basketball together. This is something nobody could have predicted, so it is really a shock for all of us now. Sometimes it is helpful to take a few minutes to talk about what this means to us all."

Validate: "Yes, it is still really difficult to even believe."

Reflect: "I remember how the death of a talented singer affected my school choir. Our next few concerts were really hard for us. How will this change in your lives affect basketball season next year?"

Empathize: "I'm very sorry that you've lost your friend. How can you support each other during this hard time?"

Help Students Help Each Other

Help students support each other outside the Safe Room. Invite them to exchange phone numbers, and encourage them to put extra energy into friendships and help each other get through the day. Remind them to take care of themselves by eating well and getting a lot of rest; share the tips on "Ways to Take Care of Yourself at Times of Loss" (page 108) and "Especially for Teens" (page 109).

The Safe Room is a place where the student can achieve an acceptance of what has happened—where child and adult can learn to trust and appreciate their shared humanity. Although the focus is on supporting the student, sharing those moments together is mutually fulfilling and beneficial. The connections established in the Safe Room transcend normal school relationships; they are beyond words and eclipse even the confines of age or gender. They approach a kind of spirituality without religion. We teach by our presence, not by our words. Modeling genuineness and creating capacity for deeper and greater awareness and understanding offer greater affirmation than words can give.

Ways to Take Care of Yourself at Times of Loss

Talk to family or friends about how you are feeling and doing.

Write your thoughts and feelings in a journal.

Write poetry.

Write letters of regret and appreciation about anything in life.

Draw pictures. Get into art.

Play a game or sport. Get a lot of exercise.

Listen to soothing music.

Listen to upbeat, rowdy music and dance!

Snack on healthy foods. Take vitamins.

Enjoy a bubble bath.

Care for your pets and house plants.

Take a favorite stuffed animal to bed with you.

Read a favorite story.

Ask someone who loves you to read you a story.

Let yourself cry.

Ask for a hug. Give a hug. Ask for another hug.

Get a lot of sleep.

Spend time in prayer or meditation.

Collect a favor from someone who owes you one.

Treat yourself to a massage.

Light a candle.

Sing loud.

Laugh. Rent a great, hilarious video. See a fun flick.

Add to this list!

Especially for Teens

Sometimes the best advice isn't advice at all. Instead, it's hearing how others felt and what they did—and then deciding whether that makes sense to you. What you'll "hear" on this page are the voices of teens who share what hurt and what helped when they had a loss in their lives. There aren't any rules for grief. What might help you in your life?

Things that helped me with my grief were . . .

- Being acknowledged. (It helped to know people were thinking of me.)

- Working. (It was often a relief to stay busy.)

- Helping others. (It made me feel part of life.)

- Sharing. (When friends told me of similar losses, I felt less alone.)

- Talking. (I was grateful for friends who were willing to listen.)

- Crying. (It helped loosen me up and brought relief.)

- Laughing. (I learned it was okay to have fun, too.)

- Hugging. (It often meant more than words could say.)

- Being with my friends. (Sometimes I like doing the old, "normal" stuff and getting away from home.)

- Being alone. (Sometimes that's what I wanted most.)

- Keeping a journal or diary. (I could write down anything I felt or thought.)

- Joining a grief support group. (Helping others also helped me feel better.)

- Writing letters of regret and appreciation to the person who died. (There were things I had to say.)

Things that hurt me were . . .

- Being avoided. (People didn't know what to say or do.)

- Being pushed to talk. (Sometimes I didn't feel like talking or didn't like people being nosy.)

- Feeling different. (People whispered about me, looked at me. Sometimes I just wanted to forget what had happened and feel normal again.)

- Being offered a replacement. (People said that I should get another dog or that my mother should have another baby.)

- Not being asked. (It hurt when people asked my friends what happened because they were afraid to ask me.)

- Being told how to feel. (I was told things like "you shouldn't cry," "don't be angry," "you should be over this by now," and "everyone feels that way.")

Things I did to help my friends with their grief were . . .

- Saying, "I'm sorry this happened to you."

- Giving a hug, bringing flowers or homemade cookies, or lending a teddy bear.

- Listening.

- Not being afraid to mention the dead person's name.

- Keeping in touch.

- Finding out if my friend wanted to do "routine" activities or wanted a break.

- Not acting embarrassed if my friend cried or laughed.

- Just being there!

—Developed by teens in the Bereavement Support Program,
Caledonia Health Care, VT

Chapter 6

Activities for the Safe Room

• • • • • • • • • • • • • • • • •

The activities in this chapter will help children, youth, and adults process loss and grief. They can be used in the classroom or in the Safe Room as needed. Most activities can be adapted for any age and used for individual or group work; training in grief therapy will help the Safe Room staff or teacher use these activities more effectively. Grief is a part of life. When the person leading the exercise is comfortable with grief as a life experience, children and youth will be comfortable expressing their own grief processes.

ACTIVITIES

Activities for Processing Grief

Consider using one or more of these activities after a death or tragedy.

1. Use clay or play dough. Some students need time to let their minds wander while the shock is wearing off. Having something for their hands to do keeps children occupied and gives their minds the freedom to let what happened sink in. Although this is especially helpful for elementary school students, it is helpful to have a variety of art supplies available for any age of students.

2. Make a giant poster. Students often want to make a poster that expresses their loss. This can be a group or individual activity. Because all schools may have at least a few students who might use this opportunity to write something inappropriate, give students 3" by 5" or 4" by 6" cards to write on, and then glue or staple those onto the banner. Otherwise, it is likely that a message will need to be cut out of the banner.

3. Draw favorite memories of the person. If there has been one or more deaths in the crisis, this activity helps students internalize the fact that their love for those who died continues and can still be a part of their lives.

4. Draw what grief is like. Use an analogy that fits the developmental age of the students to encourage them to draw pictures that represent their grief, loss, or sadness. Examples might be:

- "When someone dies, it's like we have a bucket of tears inside. Draw a picture of the bucket inside of you. How high up is the level of the tears?" There is a thorough discussion of the Lovre bucket theory in chapter 4, starting on page 77.

- "If sadness were an animal, what would it look like?"

- "If we could do all of our grieving on a special island, what would that island have on it? Draw your boat on the journey to the island."

5. Draw the transition out of grief. Some students may be struggling because they are stuck in the "isn't this awful" stage. Perhaps they are simply being a little dramatic, but most often they feel overwhelmed by grief. It takes a lot of internal work plus help and support from others to make progress during such times. Having students draw a series of three pictures can help them see where they are, where they will be, and how they can get there.

Give students blank sheets of paper, and ask them to draw a picture that shows the depth of their sadness and grief. The picture should be of the student, not of the situation. The goal is to have this be the most dramatic (even somewhat overstated) depiction of the worst part of their grief. Then provide a second sheet of paper and invite students to imagine what it could be like, some time in the future, when they have come to terms with their grief. If students protest, explain that you are not promising that everything will be okay: You are asking them to imagine what life would look like if everything was okay again. Have students place the two pictures in front of them with a space in the middle for a third picture. Ask students to show on the last sheet of paper one small thing they could do to begin to move from where they are in the first picture to where they will be in their hopeful, second picture.

ACTIVITIES

This activity helps students realize that grief is a process of many little steps: Even one step will take them closer to feeling better. Students feel empowered when they see that they can take a small step, and then another, toward feeling happy again. Inviting students to draw more pictures with additional steps gives them the opportunity to integrate concepts that will continue their movement toward control and recovery.

6. Create a treasure box of memories. Have students gather into one box things that will help them remember memories of the person who has died. The treasure box can be simple or decorated with art supplies. Students can also include items that belonged to the person who died, such as writings and pictures of the person.

7. Draw a mask of death. Masks have been used through the ages to express a variety of fears, powers, and roles. If students are old enough to understand the function of a mask and the reality of death, this activity can help them express their fears and sadness through art instead of with words. Pass out blank sheets of paper, or provide a variety of art supplies, such as clay and feathers, to allow them to create an actual mask.

8. Write private letters of regret and appreciation. Youth can process their "unfinished business" by writing about anything that is making them feel guilty about the death. Doing this permits students to make amends for past disagreements with the person who has died, and it does so without any loss of dignity. It also helps them begin to identify the wonderful things they will miss about the person. Students need to be confident that their letters will not be read by anyone else. Burning these letters can be a very cleansing release for students.

Smoke Signals

The student body president at a small rural school had died by suicide. There was no single room where all 200 students could gather at once, so we asked them to bring their notebooks and sit in the entryway and adjacent hallways of the school.

I sat in a corner that gave me eye contact with all the students, and initially I talked about how difficult it is to find words to express the emotions they felt at this time. We talked about all the different kinds of reactions they might be having—anger, guilt, sadness, and fear. After discussing the many challenges before them in dealing with their grief, I invited the students to write a letter of regret and appreciation to the boy who had died. I assured and explained to them that positively no one else would read their letters.

The hallway was extremely quiet as students bowed their heads and began to write. As the first kids finished writing, I picked up a large basket and by example I crumpled up my own letter of regret and appreciation and tossed it into the basket. The basket was passed throughout the hallway and soon all the letters were tossed in.

Then we walked into the parking lot and together we set fire to the basket, letters and all. Students spontaneously circled around the fire at a safe distance. With arms wrapped around each other's shoulders, someone began to sing a beautiful hymn that had been sung at the funeral the evening before. Others joined in. After silence settled in at the end of the hymn, others started singing other appropriate songs that everyone knew. Standing in several concentric circles, arm-in-arm, swaying back and forth to the rhythm of their songs, these students let go of some of their pain as they watched the smoke take their messages into the sky. A solemn and respectful custodian stood at the periphery with a shovel and fire extinguisher at hand.

(continued)

ACTIVITIES

Smoke Signals (continued)

Caution: If this activity is undertaken, adult supervision and safety are critical. Do not let students stand too close in case burning pieces from the container fly out from the fire. Pay attention to the construction of the basket. Those woven with tension tend to fling bits outward as they burn. Those made of stacked materials held together with twine are more apt to collapse inward safely.

---

9. Write cards and letters to the family. This is a wonderful way for youth to share their sympathy with the family. Typically, students write sincere and heartfelt messages, and they should be encouraged to share a happy memory about the deceased in words, with a picture, or both. You can also suggest that students share the attributes they most appreciated in their friend.

These letters *must be screened* by an adult to ensure that what is sent to the family is appropriate. Some students may use this activity to therapeutically work on making the event real or to come to terms with some of the event's frightening or gory details. It is possible for a well-intentioned message to carry a painful punch. In one example, a middle school boy unintentionally shot his best friend. The school gave students the opportunity to write letters both to the family of the deceased and to the boy who accidentally killed his friend. One message written by a young girl included the statement, "I know you didn't mean to murder him." Though this statement was likely well-intentioned, it could have had dreadful results had it not been caught by careful screening.

Another example illustrating the importance of screening occurred after an elementary school teacher was shot in a hunting accident by his own son. One of the students drew a picture for the cover of her card, depicting the father and the son with the deer between them. Innocently, the young artist traced the trajectory of the bullet going from the son's gun to the father's head.

In such cases, it is important to commend the student for making such a conscientious effort to understand how the tragedy could have happened. In this example, the staff member told the girl that her mother would surely also like to understand how this tragedy happened and suggested that she take her card home to show her mother. The next day when we talked about sending an uplifting message to the family, a second card was drawn by the young artist—and it was terrific.

If you face a similar situation, be certain to call the student's parents beforehand to explain the circumstances so that they are not surprised when a card that depicts the incident comes home. Spend a few minutes on the phone with them sharing a few suggestions about how they might speak with their child about loss.

10. Complete memory cards for display and the family. Copy one or both of the memory cards on page 131, or create and copy cards of your own—on cardstock if possible. Leave the cards in the Safe Room, in the office, and in other places where students can easily find them, fill them out, and drop them off. The cards can be posted on a huge, moveable bulletin board for the memory event and then given to the family of the deceased student afterwards. If you use a banner, it is better to glue or tape the cards to a large sheet of butcher paper instead of having the kids write directly on the paper—it takes only one inappropriate statement to require the cutting of a hole in the banner in order to remove it. By using separate cards, any inappropriate ones can simply be put aside. Remember: *Always screen the cards to be sure they are appropriate.*

11. Create a memory book. A memory book contains memories and mementoes of the person who died. There are many ways to use this concept. If a student dies, peers and staff could write in a book, keep it in the classroom for students to look at until the end of the year, and then invite the parent in to take it home. In cases where a student dies and leaves behind a sibling, these books can be something that the surviving sibling treasures and uses to reinterpret the loss as he or she passes through developmental stages and the loss acquires new meaning. Memory books are also very helpful for children in a family when a parent dies; as the children grow older, other people's stories in the memory book will help the children gain a fuller understanding of who the parent was as a person.

Be creative in how you use this concept. It can take several days for a memory book to circulate among everyone who wants to write in it. One way to complete a memory book in a short time is to give out high-quality sheets of paper for students and staff to fill out simultaneously. Collect the pages, and bind them into a book. Be sure to use only one size of paper to facilitate binding the pages.

12. Write grief haiku. Read several haiku to students, and talk briefly about how haiku is a traditional Japanese poetry that has three lines of 5, 7, and 5 syllables. The haiku poem does not have to be a sentence. Instead, the words in a haiku can flow together and relate to a central theme. Students can either compose their own haiku or collectively create phrases to make haiku-like expressions of their feelings, reactions, and grief.

13. Read stories about other kinds of death or loss. Such stories can have helpful insights that students can grasp in an indirect and powerful way. Depending on the story, this activity can also help students understand how a different culture handles death through ceremonies, rituals, and beliefs.

14. Design anger T-shirts. This exercise comes from Barbara Bebensee's book *Perspectives on Loss: A Manual for Educators* (1982). Give each student a copy of "My Anger T-Shirt" (page 132). Ask students to draw their anger in whatever way they want on their T-shirts. Some students may draw something abstract, while others may draw a realistic scene from a specific incident. This activity can be a good way to help students talk about something that would be too difficult for them to discuss without drawing their anger first. Invite students to share their T-shirts with others and describe the anger they have drawn.

15. Use puppets to help younger students talk about feelings and think about loss. Younger students may have an easier time talking about their feelings or thinking about loss if they can use puppets as props. Present students with a number of loss-themed story lines, and ask them to use puppets to create different endings for the stories. After students finish the stories, have them talk about the feelings their own puppet or part in the story might have had. Use their responses to talk about how there can be solutions for the problems that feelings can bring and that feelings can become better over time or can be accepted. Encourage students to think about how the loss situation may change in time by asking questions like: "Will the puppet ever want to have a new sister or brother someday?"

16. Use poetry, stories, and songs. These creative expressions can provide great ways of helping students talk about death and loss without the topic being as personal. This activity can be extended in a wonderful way by having students create their own poems, stories, or songs about death, loss, or sadness. Encourage them to include ideas about giving support, describing what helped, receiving the love of friends, and other balancing concepts.

17. Involve students in planning the memory event. Planning can occur in or out of the Safe Room. How and where planning occurs should be determined for each crisis. One option is to assign one person from the building to coordinate the planning and let students know how they can be involved.

Any memory event you plan will be more effective for students if they have a sense of ownership. Ask students who come to the Safe Room for their ideas on the most fitting tribute.

18. Create a memory bulletin board. Designate a special bulletin board in a central location that is accessible to all students (for example, in the main hallway or in the front office). Use this bulletin board to display drawings or poems students create about this tragedy. Be sure contributions are appropriate before posting them. Set a clear time (for example, after a week) when the bulletin board will be changed so that it does not become a shrine. Let students help decide what will be done with the items when it is time to change the bulletin board. One option is to invite the family members of the person who died and give the contents of the bulletin board to them.

Activities for Understanding Loss

You can use the following activities to discuss death more generally with students who visit the Safe Room or in the classroom with the empty desk. See page 112 for activities that will help students in the Safe Room process their grief after the death of someone they knew.

19. Create a lifeline. Give each student a piece of paper that is 2 or 3 feet long (newspaper publishers sometimes have remainders of newsprint rolls they will give to schools for these activities). Ask students to draw a line across the page and to write "birth" at the left edge and "today" at the right edge. The students can then write their significant life events on the line at appropriate points—times they cherish and times that were difficult. Students can do this in a variety of ways; there is no right or wrong way to represent their lives. Some will use nothing but symbols, while others will use words. Some will indicate happy events in one color and difficult events in another color. Students may not reveal some life events. For instance, someone whose family is currently going through a divorce may not be ready to reveal that. Those students who do reveal such challenges create an opportunity to discuss the losses they share with others.

Sometimes the lifelines can be posted, and all students can be encouraged to examine the milestones in each other's lives. This provides an opportunity to lead discussions about how much we all have in common, about empathy, and about the coping skills students have learned in order to survive the challenges facing them.

Lifelines also help students to begin to put loss, death, and challenges into the context of the complexities of life. This can be one of those golden "teachable moments" when students learn the larger lessons in life at a time when the meaning is personalized and coping skills can be integrated.

Teachers can use this as a group activity later in the school year to help students understand the death from a more removed perspective. Draw a line on a long piece of paper about 8 feet long. At the far left, put the beginning date of the school year, and at the far right put the last day of school (or the current date, if you are in the middle of the school year).

The elementary school version: Invite students to name all the important things that happened for them this past year. Some may recall field trips, birthdays, holidays, or funny things that happened.

If no one mentions the student who died, bring it up after many other things are on the board. For example:

> One other important thing that happened to us this year was that Billy died. That would go about here on our line. I'll write that in. . . . What do you realize when you look at our timeline when you think about Billy's death?

This statement, or something similar, will help start a short conversation about Billy's death.

The middle/high school version: Students might create a sequential list of things that have happened for them individually and collectively. It would be fine to mention national and international events, too. Student deaths would be included in much the same manner as described previously.

This activity helps students see that life is full of happy, sad, and challenging events. This is an opportunity to put death and challenges into the context of life and to reinforce the idea that death is a part of life and that there is often a balance of challenges and rewards in every year. This also helps students realize that every life is important and that people who die are not forgotten.

20. Create a "question wall." Have students write their life questions on self-stick notes or small pieces of paper. Post them on one area of a special wall designated as the "question wall." Questions that might be posted include: What is the meaning of life? What is the meaning of death? Who is God? What is nature? Who or what is part of nature? Why do we die? Why is there pain and suffering? Why do some people die young? Is there meaning to the cycle of life and dying?

Then ask the group one of the questions. As each question is answered or discussed through group dialogue or activity, remove it from that area and put it a few feet away on the same wall. As the questions are answered, the papers will move from one area to another—that way, students can look back at earlier questions as new ones are discussed.

When you have gone through their list, make a few closing comments about grief being full of questions and lessons, full of a common struggle, full of moments when we can come to know each other more deeply. Commend them for their thoughtfulness and respect for one another. End the activity by inviting students to take the paper with their question on it back, to do with as they like, or simply remove them.

21. Create a feelings list. Ask students to name their feelings. Write these feelings in a list on one side of the board. Help students make a second list on the board of what they can do to express those feelings. For example, for the feeling "anger," a student could suggest, "I could go out and beat the ground or rip newspapers."

If a student says, "I can pretend I don't have feelings," challenge the student by asking, "What happens then? What happens to those feelings, and what is the result of pretending? What will you do the next time someone you love dies?" Help the student see that burying feelings does not make them go away, and that feelings are likely to return later when the student least expects or wants them. One can also encourage youth to look for the lesson that each feeling might have for them: "My anger is one way I know how great my love is" or "How sad I am right now helps me realize how kind I want to be with my friends when they lose someone they love."

Do not expect immediate resolution of grief issues. In this type of discussion, you can also point out to students that their grief is an opportunity to decide how they will solve their problems and share serious feelings. This may be a new experience for many students. The goal is for students to identify many different kinds of feelings that are associated with loss and grief. This part of the activity demonstrates to them that they are not alone because they hear and see others list the same new or frightening feelings.

Optional: This could also be an individual activity in which each student first completes the "My Feelings" handout (page 133) by listing feelings and by coloring in areas on the outlined body where the feelings are being felt and "held." One student might color hands and feet red to represent anger, while another may color in a green tummy to show how fear makes him feel sick. Another student may color in a blue heart, indicating sadness. All the drawings will look different. The students could then share their feelings with the group through the listing activity above.

22. Create a mural. Tape huge pieces from a roll of newsprint or butcher paper on the walls, and let students create a mural of their thoughts and feelings. Take a few minutes first to guide students in realizing that anything inappropriate will be cut out of the picture. Ask if they would like to propose a common theme or if they each want to represent something that is uniquely their own statement. Sometimes telling students about how aspiring artists in Europe paint beautiful pictures on the sidewalks in chalk moves students in that direction; be sure that they realize that people will walk on the sidewalk mural and that that is part of the process—chalk is temporary! Chalk could also be used on one side of the building, depending on the siding and, of course, the permission of the administration.

23. Draw an early memory of death. Students could create one or more drawings in which they show early memories of other common life events and dilemmas (birth, first day at school, first fight with a friend, or an accomplishment).

24. Create collages about the meaning of death. Ask students to look through magazines to find, clip, and arrange images that represent what death means to them. For this activity to be most effective, ensure that students know this is not an opportunity to look for gruesome pictures. Students can make individual collages or contribute to a group collage.

25. Draw their families handling difficult times. Family drawings are wonderful for many reasons. When groups of students do these, those who have divorced parents, for example, find others who have also gone through divorce. This activity normalizes the fact that all families have struggles, and that there are many ways we handle challenges. Have students draw their families struggling with a recent challenge, loss, or disappointment. Invite them to share their pictures.

26. Create worry dolls. First, demonstrate the process for making worry dolls. (See "Worry Dolls" on pages 134–136 for instructions.)Then have students create worry dolls and containers for them as an adult reads aloud *Trouble Dolls* by Jimmy Buffett and Savannah Jane Buffett (1991). *Trouble Dolls* is long enough to give students time to make the doll and decorate the container during the reading. This activity is most effective with elementary school students.

27. Complete a loss inventory. Give each student a copy of "My Loss Inventory" (page 137). Ask students to include deaths, divorces, moves, and the many other losses that occur in life (Bebensee, 1982).

28. Do a group loss inventory. Have students volunteer verbally or write on small pieces of paper (for those who prefer anonymity) the longest list they can compile of losses and challenges. Items could include death, divorce, moves, and the death of pets. For older students, the list could include any of those plus drunk driving accidents, bullying, and so on. Allow students to add any other challenges that they face. Then you can suggest several ways to continue the activity:

- The group could rank inventory items in order of the challenge they present.

- Each student could rank items according to his or her own values and experience.

- Students could give each item a point value on a scale of 1 to 10, with 10 being those challenges that are the most difficult.

Any of these options can be very validating because they help to acknowledge the losses these youth have experienced. You can end this activity on a positive note by asking students to identify the many coping skills they have gained by surviving these losses.

29. Have discussions on death. Let each student volunteer his or her own experiences. Follow-up questions might include:

- "What did people do that was helpful?"

- "What did people do that was not helpful?"

- "What do you wish adults understood about this?"

- "Do you have unanswered questions about your experience that someone could still answer?" (These questions might relate to the cause of a particular death, where someone's ashes are, and so on.)

30. Lead a discussion on difficult issues related to death. These issues include euthanasia, life support, living wills, and so on. Set the tone for the discussion at the beginning by stating: "This is not a time to search for answers to these issues and the questions they raise. There is no right or wrong comment. Instead, this is a time to really think about the difficulties we face in these issues." Focus on this as a time students will practice respect for each other's viewpoints and allow no criticism of others. Help students struggle with the ethical challenges related to these issues. Point out that a family's religious background may predispose some students to have very strong feelings about one viewpoint or another.

31. Create a circle of listening. Have students sit in a circle. Give the first student an open-ended statement ("When I lose my jacket or pencils or lunch box, I feel . . ."). The next student repeats what the last student said and then makes his or her own statement:

> "Susie, when you lose your jacket, you feel scared. When I lose my jacket, I feel angry."

Other open-ended statements might include:

- "When I have a fight with my friend, I feel . . ."
- "When my mother or father yells at me, I feel . . ."
- "When I feel sad, something I can do to feel better is . . ."
- "If my pet died, I would feel . . ."

The goal is to keep the circle going with no one forgetting the statement of the last student to complete it.

32. Create a feelings inventory. Have students share the feelings they have experienced when they learned of someone's death. List these feelings on the board or on a piece of butcher paper, and be sure the list includes at least one item from each student. Validate the range of emotional responses to death.

33. Draw a tree of life. There are several options for this activity.

Option 1: Draw a huge tree trunk with roots and bare branches on the board or a piece of butcher paper. Ask students to label the roots with the things people need for a healthy life (food, shelter, water, love, kindness, and so on). Then let the students draw the leaves on the tree, labeling them with the results of having the nurturing from the roots (happiness, health, friendships, strength, and so on.) Ask them, "What will the tree look like if there aren't enough nutrients for the roots?"

Option 2: Have students draw their own tree of life and in some way represent their own families and losses. Be flexible in how students do this. Some may use the tree concept differently and reveal other kinds of insights. For example, some students might draw the tree with branches or leaves that represent people who are still living and with leaves that have fallen to the ground to represent those who have died.

Caution: Consider whether you know the students' histories well enough for them to benefit from creating individual trees. Adopted children, youth who recently immigrated from war-torn countries, or students from families in strife may find this activity too painful if they are not in a counseling setting.

Planning for Loss and Grief
Activities Checklist

● ● ● ● ● ● ● ● ● ● ● ● ● ● ● ● ● ●

Use the planning chart below to identify the activities you may use. Complete the chart by planning what you will need for the activities and how you will present them. Use the materials column as a checklist to help you gather supplies before you do the activity.

Activity Number and Name	Materials Needed

The Safe Room • Copyright © 2006 by Cheri Lovre
Solution Tree • www.solution-tree.com

Memory Cards

• • • • • • • • • • • • • • • • • •

What I most appreciated about _____ **was . . .**

My favorite memory of _____ **is . . .**

My Anger T-Shirt

My Feelings

• • • • • • • • • • • • • • • • •

Here are some of the feelings I have:

Here is where I hold those feelings in my body:

_____

_____

_____

_____

_____

_____

_____

_____

_____

_____

_____

_____

_____

_____

_____

_____

_____

_____

Worry Dolls

Materials

__ One pipe cleaner per student

__ Colored yarn and other items for decoration

__ Optional: one match box (or small container) per student

Preparation

1. Cut one pipe cleaner into two pieces for each student:
   - 1½" piece
   - 4" piece

2. Place yarn, other items for decoration, and match boxes out for the students.

Instructions

1. Bend long pipe cleaner in half over the end of a pencil so it is rounded.

2. Twist twice to create the head.

3. Place short pipe cleaner as arms under the twisted part, and twist the arms around once so the short pipe cleaner is attached to the long one.

4. Below the arms, twist the two ends of the long pipe cleaner a few more times for the body. Wrap in little pieces of yarn for clothes.

5. Leave some length for legs. Pull the legs apart a little to shape the human.

6. Add hair or decorations to the worry doll.

7. Optional: If students have match boxes, invite students to decorate the boxes for their worry doll to "live" in.

Instructions for Students

1 Bend long pipe cleaner in half over the end of a pencil so that it is rounded.

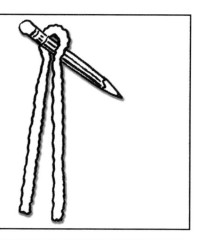

2 Twist twice to create the head.

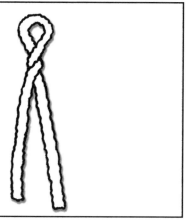

3 Place short pipe cleaner (the arms) under the head, and twist the arms around once to attach the short pipe cleaner to the long one.

4 Below the arms, twist the two ends of the long pipe cleaner a few more times to create the body. Wrap in little pieces of yarn for clothes.

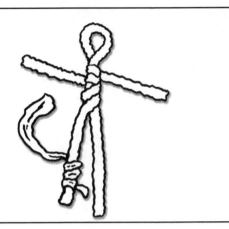

5 Leave some length for legs. Pull the legs apart a little to make the worry doll look more lively.

6 Add hair or decorations to the worry doll.

The Safe Room • Copyright © 2006 by Cheri Lovre
Solution Tree • www.solution-tree.com

My Loss Inventory

Write down the losses you have had in your life in the first column. Then rate how much you were affected by these losses on a scale of 1 to 10, with 1 for not at all and 10 for very much.

Loss (death, divorce, moving, other)	How great was the loss?	How sad or hurt were you when it happened?	How sad or hurt are you now?

Chapter 7

Unique and Difficult Circumstances

• • • • • • • • • • • • • • • • • •

Every crisis has its own unique dimensions. Considering all the difficult circumstances that we face in our modern world, selecting information to include in this chapter is not an easy task. Therefore, only a few of the more common challenges—suicide, homicide, other violent deaths, and abductions—will be explored here.

It is impossible to prepare for every possibility, but having a thorough general crisis response plan and well-trained staff is an excellent beginning. These will serve a school and its students well during difficult and unpredictable times when combined with flexibility, integration of newly learned lessons, and the continuous honing of crisis team and Safe Room staff expertise.

Suicide

Suicide—simply discussing the subject with students intimates extraordinary challenges.

Sometimes it is feared that simply asking a student if he or she is suicidal will plant the idea. There are many students who have contemplated or attempted suicide, but talking about suicide with students does not make them consider it for themselves for the first time. In fact, letting students know that an adult is not afraid to listen to the truth about their feelings creates an opportunity to discuss deeper issues, and that is definitely a good thing if handled by a well-trained person.

Until school staff becomes comfortable talking about suicide, some individuals will harbor fears that mere mention of the subject will put students at risk. Some schools have been reluctant to initiate Safe Rooms in the aftermath of a student death due to suicide. It is important that schools do only what the administrators feel competent and prepared to support. In making that decision, administrators may want to consider the following issues.

Legal Implications

Understand that suicide is a legal determination with many consequences. Police may be unable to determine whether a death was suicide for days or even weeks following the incident. Care must be taken with any announcements, and clear messages about content must be given to teachers before they lead discussions in their classrooms. The information and wording contained in those "clear messages" is a decision best made by a knowledgeable group and not by just one individual.

For this and other reasons, including potential liability, it is recommended that any written memos to staff, comments to the press, or official announcement to students not label the death as a suicide—even if the family uses that term. Later, the family may regret their choice of words. Administrators should be certain, when they discuss the death in an official context, to indicate how the *family* refers to the incident, without using the word "suicide": "John's family called to tell us that they believe he died from a gunshot wound." In some cases, it may be preferable not to mention the mode of death at all: "John's family called to tell us that he died this morning."

Terminology

Even when the official school announcement and any written references to the death do not contain the word "suicide," students are likely to ask questions about the manner of death. In unofficial discussions in classrooms and in the Safe Room, teachers and staff can respond in more depth to the issue of suicide, but be certain that all staff know how to use language that does not glorify the mode of death. The American Foundation for Suicide Prevention (AFSP) recommends that we say that someone has "died by suicide," rather than has "committed suicide" or "is a suicide." That phrasing, the AFSP suggests, may reduce the person to the mode of death or connote criminal or sinful behavior. The term "committed" may also suggest the successful

Creating a Comfort Zone

Several years ago, a mother called me because she was very concerned about her daughter. Her daughter had pulled away from friends, lost interest in academics and athletic pursuits, and was withdrawn from usual parent-daughter communication. The mother was certain her daughter was contemplating suicide, and I agreed to see the teenager.

After about 10 minutes into the session, I sensed that something else was going on. So I asked, "Do you know why your parents brought you in?"

The student shrugged. "I figure because I'm growing up and becoming more independent. I can dress how I want to, and sometimes I hang out with kids my parents don't like."

"Actually," I said, "your mother is afraid you're thinking about hurting yourself. She wonders if you're suicidal."

The adolescent's face and entire presence shifted noticeably, and a wry but animated smile crossed her lips. "She does? Well, actually, I'm not talking to her much because I don't know what to say to her—I'm not suicidal, but I think I might be pregnant!" I quickly assured her that although teen pregnancy wasn't my professional area of expertise, I could find her help and support.

Because of our discussion, things moved forward, and we invited the student's mother back into the room. Soon, both mom and daughter reached out to each other, addressing the situation together and giving mutual support. They took down contact information for local resources and were quickly on their way.

In this experience, asking the student if she was suicidal did not create suicidal feelings or "make" her suicidal. But my willingness to talk with the young woman about something as serious as suicide did help her feel safe enough to unburden her real problem.

completion of an act, which would send the wrong message to send those at risk of suicide. Along those lines, it is better to refer to "nonfatal attempts" than "unsuccessful" or "failed" attempts at suicide.

Staff and Teacher Needs

Prepare teachers to deal with the inevitable questions that will arise. It may be appropriate to coach teachers to ask students what they have heard, so that the students will "lay everything on the table."

When the official announcement says only that there has been a death in the school community, but students say in class that they have heard that the death was a suicide, teachers can start a discussion to clarify rumors and take the focus off the mode of death:

Teacher: "How many of you had already heard about John's death? What have you heard?"

Student: "My mom is his mom's friend, and we know that he killed himself."

Teacher: "Frequently, students have news or information that school staff doesn't have yet. But we also know that even when a death looks like a suicide, it often takes police several days to investigate and determine for sure that it truly was intentional. We don't have that information from police at the current time.

"One of our greatest needs when someone we care about dies is to understand the causes and details of the death.

We'll know more about that over the next few days as the investigation progresses. In the meantime, it is really important for us not to spread rumors, conjecture, or assumptions. I know this is really difficult, because we really want to know. What is it like for all of you when what the family says, or what the school says, doesn't add up to what you have heard from other sources?"

At this point, the teacher can redirect the discussion from arguing about whether the death really was a suicide to expressing how difficult it is when facts do not add up or when we do not know all of the truth and information about a death early on. The goal is to shift the focus from conjecture about the past to what those present are feeling right now:

Teacher: "Part of coming to terms with a death or loss is understanding exactly what happened. We will all feel differently if we learn that it really was a cry for help and John didn't mean to die, or if we learn that it was an accident while he was cleaning a gun. Knowing how someone dies helps us grieve and come to terms with the loss. What is it like for you at this point, when we still don't know everything?"

It is very helpful to validate students' struggle with those feelings of uncertainty. They have the opportunity to learn that death and grieving are not about blame: They do not have to make the school or the family right or wrong. They benefit by simply learning how to live with ambiguity without assigning guilt or blame.

Sometimes we think—it is wishful thinking—that if we do not talk with students about suicide and other difficult topics, then they will not discuss these things among themselves. However, the reality is they will talk about these issues whether we bring them up or not, and it is preferable for them to be talking with adult supervision than without it.

In one instance, for example, a young high school student died by suicide, but the family did not want to call it suicide. This is not uncommon; sometimes this reluctance is the result of the family's feelings of shame and guilt, and other times it is the result of misguided efforts to protect other students. In this particular case, the boy shot himself, and students were aware that he died from a gunshot wound. Because the family did not want their son's death to be called a suicide, rumors soon circulated that the boy's stepfather was getting away with murder. When the family began to understand the consequences of their secrecy, they were willing to express the truth concerning their child's death.

It can be very helpful if the Flight Team outlines a script or guideline that teachers can follow to acknowledge the wide array of information and misinformation being broadcast concerning a recent death. The outline should help teachers focus classroom discussions on the angst students are feeling, rather than on the circumstances surrounding the death.

Student Needs

Those who have lost a friend to suicide will display the same kinds of grief associated with any other kind of death, but usually additional emotions are involved, too, such as guilt and fear.

When Safe Rooms are available during the aftermath of a suicide, staff can often identify other students who might be suicidal as well as help those who are simply struggling to manage their emotions. Those emotions will still be present when a Safe Room is *not* available.

It is important, therefore, if a school decides not to open a Safe Room after a suicide, to find other means to assist students in the healthy expression of grief, anger, anxiety, and guilt. If the family is having a funeral that is not private, for example, often students will benefit by attending. This does not necessarily assist in closure at the school level, but will have some of that apparent effect for individual students who attend. Once again, schools need to do what they most feel prepared to do. Recognize, however, that ignoring the death will not prevent students from talking about it. Not providing help does not mean that students do not need help.

Safe Room Advantages

Following a suicide, it is important to accept and validate student fears, anger, and guilt to help students move toward a more positive focus. Safe Room staff can:

- Listen for clues of suicidal thoughts.

- Help students understand that no single individual can cause someone to commit suicide, nor can one single individual prevent someone from committing suicide.

- Help students understand that decisions people make about suicide are the result of complex social actions and many other variables, and are not ordinarily triggered by *one person* or *one event*.

- Encourage students to tell an adult if they are concerned about a friend or about themselves.

- Pay special attention to close friends of the deceased and to any students who have lost a family member to suicide.

School responses to death by suicide, deaths that remain unsolved, or deaths that involve the unraveling of secrets are more difficult than school responses to more common deaths. There are no easy answers, but Safe Rooms allow schools to identify students at risk, clarify facts (those that are known and have been authorized to be given out), decrease rumors, and guide student conversations in a positive framework.

Homicide

The murder of someone students know strips them of a feeling of safety. It assaults their sense of security, violates their innocence, and breeds fear and guilt. If the perpetrator has not been caught, students may fear that others they know will be killed. If the perpetrator was known to the victim, some students may wonder, "Could someone I love turn crazy and murder me or someone else?" Students may also feel guilty: "It should have been me. He *[or she]* was a better student *[or better friend, better athlete, and so on]* than I am." There is the likelihood of great indignation, anger, and rage about the unfairness of the death within the school community as a whole.

Safe Room Tasks

There are several issues that Safe Room staff must address following a homicide:

1. Reassure students of their safety. Students need practical and realistic assurance about their safety both at school and in the "real world." The primary reassurance students need is to know that very few people become "so sick and disturbed" that they commit murder. Explain that this was a very rare occurrence. This is especially important if the perpetrator was the child's parent or family member.

2. Provide accurate information about the case. Police can clarify the facts of the death and increase students' sense of security that all that can be done is being done. Be aware, however, that having police on campus may either calm students or intensify the sense of danger among students—even if they are only visiting to make a presentation. Listen to students and act accordingly.

3. Assess students' mental and physical health. Find out whether students are having nightmares or difficulty concentrating because their thoughts are obsessed with the event. To accurately assess student needs, get assistance from someone trained in trauma.

4. Provide ongoing support. Students may need support for a long time after a homicide, depending on their relationship with the victim and the circumstances of the crime. Safe Room staff should consult regularly with the Flight Team leader to ensure opportunities are not missed that would provide helpful support to staff, students, and parents. Consider using experienced professionals from local mental health agencies, the youth services team, children's services, and so on to provide long-term support.

Repercussions for Abused Students

Incidents of homicide will often trigger new fears among those students who suffer domestic violence or abuse in their own homes. They might ask, "Could this happen in my home?" It is better to give students a safe environment to voice their concerns than to allow them to slip into deeper fear and depression as a result of their anxiety over secrets and unspoken issues.

Those who have experienced physical abuse in their homes will appear agitated and anxious if they are worried about their parents being capable of murder. It is important to refer students who are ill at ease to a counselor to assure proper assessment and care. Students may need outside support to help them separate fear, possibility, and reality. Help students at risk for abuse to identify who they could call when things seem out of control. Consider involving mental health agencies, children's services, or others who have expertise in child abuse. Remember our obligation to follow reporting laws!

Other Violent Deaths

Following a death caused by carelessness, drunk driving, or a violent act, special measures to support and protect the friends of the perpetrator may be needed, both in the Safe Room and in the school environment in general. Siblings of the perpetrator and any groups or clubs the perpetrator belonged to might also be targeted by other students. Often, a sense of unfairness about a death creates a desire to blame, and those peers who are friends with the student who caused the death may be added into the blame mix. Sometimes there is a noticeable "dissing" or isolation of those peers. In some cases, these students could be bullied or beaten up by others.

It is important not only to protect these students' physical and emotional well-being, but also to give teachers language and concepts to use when addressing all of their students. It may be necessary to state the obvious, to clearly articulate student assumptions, and to elaborate on why they are unfair:

Teacher: "Sometimes when we are angry about a death, we look for anyone at all to blame. We may try to blame others just by association—because they knew the person who caused the death. But wouldn't it seem unfair to you, if you were blamed for something that someone else did? To make schools a safer and kinder place, we have to rise above our anger and do what is fair and just, and that would not include blaming others by association."

Abductions

While Safe Rooms most often serve the needs of students after a death, they can also be helpful after other events that bring out student fears, such as when a child is missing. In these situations, if a district decides not to have a Safe Room for any reason, administrators must identify alternative ways to offer assistance to those students who need it.

With abductions, a variety of factors—such as whether the child knew the abductor, whether the abductor has been caught, whether the abductor broke into the home, what the abducted student's home situation was like—can influence the dynamic in the school and how Safe Room staff should respond to student fears and questions.

Was the Abductor Known to the Child?

If the abductor was known to the child who is missing—an estranged parent, for instance—reassure students that although what the abductor has done is against the law and may be causing incredible anguish for the rest of the family, we can nevertheless assume or hope that the child will be cared for and unharmed. The challenge is to reassure students about their friend's likelihood of safety, without appearing to reinforce or accept the behavior of the person taking the child.

Some students who come into the Safe Room may turn up there because of their own fears that an angry, estranged parent might do something very harmful to them. In such instances, it may be best to turn them over directly to the school counselor. The counselor may be more familiar with the student's situation and will have a better opportunity for assessing the student's actual level of risk. He or she can also make the best decisions concerning intervention or agency involvement.

Has the Abductor Been Caught?

If the abductor is unknown to the community and continues to be at large, this will often bring about great levels of concern for students in regard to their own safety. Helpful measures might include bringing in police to talk with students about safety; they might recommend that students walk to and from school with buddies, offer advice on selecting safe routes of travel, and outline other safety tips.

Parents, too, will have fears and concerns. This is a good time for parent meetings with police (who can offer parents safety tips and information) and with school administrators (who can reassure parents on existing and new safety measures the school is putting into place). Listen to parent concerns, and further adapt school policies and procedures to the needs of the situation.

Did the Abductor Break Into a Home?

In these instances, fear is likely to spread throughout much of the student population and include parents, as well. The more information the school can provide on safety and coping skills, the more students and parents will trust the school. Administrators can use their ability to contact parents; consider offering the school facility as a place where community experts can speak at parent meetings.

Other Disappearances

There are many ways that children can disappear without abduction being a likely cause, such as becoming lost on a hike in a wilderness area. Unusual dynamics result from this kind of event.

Casting Blame

Both students and parents tend to blame others during such circumstances. Students may blame the parents for letting the child go on the hike or not staying close enough to him or her, while parents might blame the search-and-rescue team for being unable to find the missing child.

Blame tends to reassure us that "it couldn't happen to me." If adults can convince themselves that the parents were at fault for not keeping an eye on the child, they can also reassure themselves that as parents, *they* certainly would never allow that to happen.

It can be helpful to carefully listen to the blaming statement, and then to state the obvious: that sometimes we blame others to reassure ourselves. Then move the conversation along to help students and parents identify times when they were blamed for things that others did not fully understand.

Present or Past Tense?

One of the greatest challenges with missing children is deciding how long to speak of the child as still living and when to move to past tense. The message is very clear when you say, "Billy was a good friend," rather than "Billy is your good friend."

There is often no single moment when the students, staff, and family are all ready to use past tense in referring to a missing child. In cases such as these, there are no "rules" for how to handle the situation, only cautions: People need time to think deeply about how to address each aspect of the situation. It may not be a uniform transition from past to present tense. There will likely be many discussions and conversations all year long about this issue.

The Empty Desk

A few years ago, an elementary student was on a hike with his church youth group and did not return with the rest of the party. A search was mounted immediately, but the wilderness area spanned hundreds of miles, and by evening, the missing boy had not been found. Authorities were quickly involved, and many teams of search-and-rescue volunteers began the long process of looking for the boy.

For the first few weeks, it was difficult to get any students from the boy's school to devote attention to academics. Weeks later, the uncertainty about the missing boy was conspicuous. The teacher decided not to remove the missing boy's desk until the students brought it up and asked for it to be moved. The child went missing in September, and the desk was still in place through early spring. At that point, students asked to have it moved into a corner of their room, where they used it to do their homework. They were very clear with the teacher that the missing child's desk was not to be used as a place to give students a time-out.

Later in the spring, students asked that the desk be moved to the hallway, just outside the door. Their feeling was, "We would want him to see it right away if he came back, so he'd know that we've all been waiting for him."

It appeared classmates were slowly coming to terms with the missing boy's death, and moving his desk a little further away from the mainstream of the classroom bore witness to this feeling. At the end of the year, the school had a Celebration of Friendship to pay tribute to the missing boy's importance in their lives, without addressing the question of whether he was alive or dead. When his bones were found a year later, the school had a memory event.

It is really helpful, in the Safe Room and in the school as a whole, to be open about how difficult it is when we do not know the facts. When we know what happened, we can begin to deal with it, to cope, and to make whatever meaning we can of the loss. But when someone is missing, these essential tasks of grief cannot be completed.

Returning Personal Belongings

The subject of the deceased student's belongings may be brought up by students in the Safe Room. Close friends may wish to have a keepsake; others may want to play a role in returning the deceased student's items to the family. Team members need to be sensitive in the disposition and handling of any of the person's belongings. These are the family's treasures and must be treated with dignity and returned in that spirit. If students request a keepsake, first make a positive comment to reaffirm their friendship, then point out the family's needs and role, and finally suggest a way to reconcile the two:

Teacher or Safe Room staff member: "It is a wonderful tribute to your friendship that you want to remember Lisa. Her parents will probably want to come to school or have us take her belongings to them. We're going to write cards and letters to her family today. Would you like help in writing a letter to them that you'd like something to remember Lisa by? We don't know what the family will decide, but it will probably mean a lot to them that you care this much."

If the student who has died shared a locker with someone else, consideration must also be extended to the locker partner.

However, typically there is no rush in returning the deceased student's belongings to the family. It can be a wonderful experience to invite the family to come to the school—when they are ready—to receive their child's belongings and the school's condolences.

A Message of Love

Joey, a middle school student, died in a car accident while on a weekend trip with friends of the family. Joey was average academically, but he excelled in basketball. His locker partner, Mike, was also on the basketball team. Joey's parents and Mike were asked how they would like to handle getting Joey's things out of his locker. They decided to meet at the locker after all the other students had left the building and to go through the locker together. Mike had a wonderful touch. He removed the photos, notes, and drawings Joey had taped on the inside of the locker door one by one, telling Joey's parents something about each item: what each photo had meant to Joey, what musical groups he liked, and other students Joey had known and liked. Taped to the locker was even a very special handwritten note from Joey's mother, encouraging him to do well on an upcoming test. She had slipped it into his book bag several weeks earlier, and Joey had saved it, little knowing she would see how much it had meant to him.

In the case of a missing student, remember, there is no need to rush to mention student belongings to the family. One of the parents may ask about the child's desk or locker eventually, and that is a great time to deal with it. If the child's family does not bring up the subject, the school can wait for some time, even until the end of the year. At some point, though, be certain the family knows that the school has all of the student's things and that the family can decide how the school will handle them—to leave them in the locker or desk, to pack them up and save them for the family, to deliver them to the home, or to have the family come to the school to collect them.

Coping with the ambiguity of unique and difficult circumstances can be very challenging. When a child goes missing or a trusted friend or family member commits an unthinkable act, adults struggle to cope with their own emotions, much less to help students cope with their fear and uncertainty. The most important thing we can do as adults to help students, however, is simply to respond. When we bring up the subject of the abduction, death, or other event and show our own grief, we model to students that their feelings are a natural response to loss. When we cannot find the right words, we can always listen—and that may be what students need most.

Afterword

Responding With Heart

At times of crisis, take a deep breath, and consider the bigger picture. Use many heads to make decisions, and—when possible—take time to make sensitive decisions, rather than rushing into something that is not well–thought out. Have a philosophy, a plan, guidelines, and procedures—and then be prepared to amend the plan to meet the needs of each unique situation. The sheer unpredictability of death and loss demands training, practice, and flexibility. There are more kinds of unique and challenging circumstances than could ever be addressed here.

Schools often feel overwhelmed by these challenges. "Let's keep our crisis response small and manageable," some argue. But the most expedient response in the short term is not necessarily the most efficient in the long term. When we address our students' real needs, the school community heals more quickly after a crisis, and everyday school climate improves. In the aftermath of tragedy, a school is better able to maintain its primary function—classroom teaching—when it provides a viable alternative for those students who are temporarily wounded by a significant loss. Learning still takes place in the Safe Room. There, students grow to understand some painful truths about life and to appreciate the deep comfort that comes from empathy and caring. In the process, they gain coping skills they will use the rest of their lives.

THE SAFE ROOM

The Safe Room is the heart of your crisis response, and children intuitively appreciate the care and support shown there, as illustrated in this closing story from a rural town. In this small community, students knew each other, and many were also related. The town had only one school to serve grades K–8 and no high school of its own. When early rumors of a shooting reached residents, panic spread: Who would be next? Were the children safe? The postmistress ushered customers off the street and locked them into her office while they waited for news. When they learned that an estranged father had shot and killed his wife and three children (and then himself), everyone was devastated.

The next day, the Safe Room at the small school was packed. Students sat on the floor in groups of eight, each child on his or her own square of carpet. Supported by Safe Room staff members (who all happened to be women that day), the children solemnly debated what these deaths meant to them and how the father could do that to his family. Discussion alternated with intervals of quiet reflection. Eventually, a third grader in pigtails and overalls reached up and patted the knee of the Safe Room staff member sitting with her group and said, "You know, I'm really glad you brought your ladies' club to our school today."

That is how a Safe Room should feel to students—not like a room filled with clinical professionals, but like a room filled with caring adults. In its most basic form, a Safe Room is about making this kind of gentle, informal, loving connection with grieving students. For them, the Safe Room provides a warm, welcoming shelter from the storms of life—a chance to restore themselves before the arduous journey ahead.

References and Resources

References

Bebensee, B. (1982). *Perspectives on loss: A manual for educators.* Evergreen, CO: Author.

Buffett, J., & Buffett, S. J. (1991). *Trouble dolls.* San Diego, CA: Harcourt Brace.

Wolfelt, A. (1983). *Helping children cope with grief.* Muncie, IN: Accelerated Development.

Wolfelt, A. (1992). *Understanding grief: Helping yourself heal.* Muncie, IN: Accelerated Development.

Wolfelt, A. (1997). *The journey through grief: Reflections on healing.* Fort Collins, CO: Companion Press.

Resources

Hospice

Caring Connections: www.caringinfo.org

Hospice Foundation of America: www.hospicefoundation.org

Hospice Net: www.hospice net.org

Suicide

American Association of Suicidology: www.suicidology.org

American Foundation for Suicide Prevention: www.afsp.org

Centre for Suicide Prevention (Canada): www.suicideinfo.ca

Suicide Awareness Voices of Education: www.save.org

Trauma

International Society for Traumatic Stress Studies: www.istss.org

Eye Movement Desensitization and Reprocessing (EMDR) Institute: www.emdr.com

Green Cross Foundation: www.greencross.org

Academy of Traumatology: www.traumatologyacademy.org

Make the Most of Your Professional Development Investment

Let Solution Tree (formerly National Educational Service) schedule time for you and your staff with leading practitioners in the areas of:

- **Professional Learning Communities** with Richard DuFour, Robert Eaker, Rebecca DuFour, and associates
- **Effective Schools** with associates of Larry Lezotte
- **Assessment *for* Learning** with Rick Stiggins and associates
- **Crisis Management and Response** with Cheri Lovre
- **Classroom Management** with Lee Canter and associates
- **Discipline With Dignity** with Richard Curwin and Allen Mendler
- **SMART School Teams** with Jan O'Neill and Anne Conzemius
- **PASSport to Success** (parental involvement) with Vickie Burt
- **Peacemakers** (violence prevention) with Jeremy Shapiro

Additional presentations are available in the following areas:

- At-Risk Youth Issues
- Bullying Prevention/Teasing and Harassment
- Team Building and Collaborative Teams
- Data Collection and Analysis
- Embracing Diversity
- Literacy Development
- Motivating Techniques for Staff and Students

Solution Tree
304 W. Kirkwood Avenue
Bloomington, IN 47404-5131
(812) 336-7700
(800) 733-6786 (toll-free number)
FAX (812) 336-7790
www.solution-tree.com

NEED MORE COPIES OR ADDITIONAL RESOURCES ON THIS TOPIC?

Need more copies of this book? Want your own copy? Need additional resources on this topic? If so, you can order additional materials by using this form or by calling us toll free at (800) 733-6786 or (812) 336-7700. Or you can order by FAX at (812) 336-7790 or visit our web site at www.solution-tree.com.

Title	Price*	Quantity	Total
The Safe Room	$ 17.95		
Anger Management for Youth	24.95		
Building Classroom Communities	9.95		
Crisis Resource Manual	55.00		
Media Relations Guide	12.00		
Peacemakers (curriculum)	169.00		
Teaching Empathy (book and music CD)	34.95		
Teasing and Harassment	9.95		
		SUBTOTAL	
		SHIPPING	
Continental U.S.: Please add 6% of order total. Outside continental U.S.: Please add 8% of order total.			
		HANDLING	
Continental U.S.: Please add $4. Outside continental U.S.: Please add $6.			
		TOTAL (U.S. funds)	

*Price subject to change without notice.

❏ Check enclosed ❏ Purchase order enclosed
❏ Money order ❏ VISA, MasterCard, Discover, or American Express (circle one)

Credit Card No._____ Exp. Date_____
Cardholder Signature _____

SHIP TO:
First Name_____ Last Name_____
Position _____
Institution Name_____
Address_____
City_____ State_____ ZIP_____
Phone_____ FAX_____
E-mail _____

Solution Tree (formerly National Educational Service)
304 W. Kirkwood Avenue
Bloomington, IN 47404-5131
(812) 336-7700 • (800) 733-6786 (toll-free)
FAX (812) 336-7790
e-mail: orders@solution-tree.com
www.solution-tree.com

Solution Tree